INTERNATIONAL PUBLISHERS
381 Park Avenue South New York, N. Y. 10016

Apartheid

A COLLECTION OF WRITINGS
ON SOUTH AFRICAN RACISM
BY SOUTH AFRICANS

BY THE EDITOR

A Walk in the Night
And A Threefold Cord
The Stone Country
In the Fog of the Season's End

Apartheid

A COLLECTION OF WRITINGS ON SOUTH AFRICAN RACISM BY SOUTH AFRICANS

Alex La Guma
EDITOR

INTERNATIONAL PUBLISHERS
NEW YORK

Published simultaneously by
International Publishers, New York,
Lawrence and Wishart, London and
Seven Seas Books, Berlin, 1971
Second printing by International Publishers,
New York and Seven Seas Books, Berlin, 1978

Acknowledgements

The compiler of this volume wishes to express his sincere appreciation and admiration for the publishers who exercised extreme patience while waiting for the manuscript. The editor of *Sechaba,* official organ of the African National Congress, South Africa, is thanked for permission to use the articles, "The Development of the South African Revolution", "The Freedom Charter", and "Strategy and Tactics of the South African Revolution". A special mark of appreciation goes to Pam Flintoff and Maggie Lockwood who did most of the typing.

Copyright (c) Seven Seas Books 1971
ISBN 0-7178-0332-5
Cover Design by Lothar Reher
Printed in the German Democratic Republic

Hilltop Ruins and Tall Walls:
Two Poems for Freedom Fighters

Midsummer Sleep and Zimbabwe Battlefield

Listening grey with seed-spill
It is high time a low spirit
Fell and crawled where the weeds fell
Lie low-crept like some slinking ferret
Spying out the land well
Sunk into the soil till
The earth with ears inherit
Can broadcast and all tell
Where the first who stir it
Still made fertile drill
By mark time their green cell
We shall mark it, disinter it
When morning is lustrousness on the pearl shell
Now pour it.

Cosmo Pieterse

In Man Lies All His Revolution

for B. F.—who may have died
near the Zimbabwe River

February
Each young man dead
    in your youth
    every new year
    every
February briefly refracts our climates and seasons
    for your skull covers various
        dimensions different
            hemisphere comradely
                for comeliness
   is the flagrant bed
    of the mourning sheets
      the yellow
            seeds
  fallow   in the ripe brain
    but by the feather-arrow
      forensically
        logistically
           done to death
              bullet
                  showering you from your
                      splintered head
                  brothering the flower
                    we wear
                      brother
                  we swear
                        LIFE
              Basil.

                Cosmo Pieterse

CONTENTS

INTRODUCTION

In the course of addressing numerous meetings called for the purpose of explaining apartheid and its effects to audiences in the United Kingdom and abroad, I have often been faced by incredulous people who expressed doubts about the shocking truth of racism in South Africa. Surely you must be exaggerating? Certainly it can't be really as bad as all that? No doubt people could have expressed similar incredulity about Nazi Germany when told that soap had been manufactured from the fat of victims of the concentration camps. Truth is often surprising; the truth about racism is more often than not staggering.

South Africa has not sent "inferior" peoples to gas ovens and therefore it is assumed that the concentration camp, the classical institution of fascism, does not exist in our country. Genocide is not necessarily a process of instant mass extermination. On 11 November 1969 the English-language "opposition" paper, *The Rand Daily Mail*, carried a feature article dealing with the appalling conditions in one of the Government's "Bantu Homelands". "As 'Black Spot' removals bring more and more people to an already depressed part of the Tswana Bantustan, malnutrition diseases and plain starvation increase. Of 22 children who died recently in the area's only general hospital, 13 were suffering from malnutrition or starvation."

"Tens of thousands of rootless African women, old people and fatherless children were plucked from their homes and left to rot in their resettlement villages, the names of some of which still stink in the nostrils of decency," Mr. J. Hamilton Russell, South African M. P., said in Cape Town. "Visits are not encouraged to these so-called resettlement villages, made up first of tents, then small corrugated iron shanties, then finally cramped concrete huts, always overcrowded and in which human beings live in deplorable conditions." Another report, early in 1970, states: "About 54,000 people are being moved from Alexandra Township (near Johannesburg). The township will be turned into a hostel town housing 30,000 'single' African men and women."

The people of South Africa have therefore a special interest in the struggle to overthrow apartheid. Nowhere else today is racialism so blatantly and unashamedly embraced, so brutally imposed and enforced.

Racism in South Africa, the ideology of White supremacy and Black inferiority, was given birth by White settlers who invaded our country in the seventeenth century. During the seventeenth, eighteenth and nineteenth centuries the Whites carried out their policy of incursions, theft, fraud and aggression against the African people. They met with firm resistance. In the Cape alone there were nine wars of resistance against this encroachment waged over a period of one hundred years. After a series of grim battles, resistance was eventually subdued by superior firepower. Even after their defeat the Africans did not readily and voluntarily surrender their sought-after labour to the Whites, and numerous devices, many originating in the days of slavery, are still used to compel them to work. Amongst these heavy taxation in relation to meagre earnings and the pass laws (permit to work or live in an area) feature prominently. The pass laws comprise an intricate and devilish system the complications of which even the African people, the direct victims, find difficult to comprehend.

The discovery of gold and diamonds laid the foundation for racial discrimination in industry. The original skilled workers in the mines were Whites who came from Europe. Africans were employed in the more arduous labour as unskilled workers. This system proved profitable to mine owners and indeed to all capital in South Africa. The White aristocracy of labour is bribed to support the system of racism with better working conditions and higher salaries. The mining industry is also a marriage between international capital and local feudalism.

In a burst of frankness, the pioneer imperialist, Cecil John Rhodes, said in the Cape House of Assembly: "I will lay down my policy on this Native question ... either you receive them on an equal footing as citizens or call them a subject race ... I have made up my mind that there must be class (race) legislation ... The Native is to be treated as a child and denied the franchise. We must adopt the system of despotism such as works well in India in our relations with the barbarians of South Africa ... These are my politics and these are the politics of South Africa." A modern prototype, Mr. Con Botha, Nationalist Member of the Provincial Council for Newcastle, recently told a Natal audience that, "... if Africans are forbidden to live in the same area, they are foolish to get married, and if they committed this folly, they and not the laws are at fault."

The legal cornerstone of racism in South Africa was laid when Britain vested all the political power in the hands of the White minority in 1910. The constitution legalised racism and prepared the ground for all the aspects of national oppression, exploitation, humiliation and brutalisation of the non-White people. Given these favourable conditions, South Africa has become the hunting ground of international capitalism. Superficially the country is ruled by White South Africans. In essence, however, the power rests with the South African monopolists and the international consortium of imperialism. The combination of racialism, capitalism and international imperialism has made South Africa a colony of a special type.

The majority of the people, the non-Whites, are subjected to the worst forms of colonial subjection; they are neither independent nor free. They are landless, voteless and compelled to provide cheap labour to produce the fabulous wealth which is bargained for in the stock markets of Johannesburg, London and New York.

"The total value of foreign investment in South Africa amounted to $4,802 million at the end of 1965 ... The United Kingdom held almost three-fifths of all foreign investments. The United States with 12 per cent had the second largest South African holdings. The investments of international organisations, French and Swiss investors represented between 4 and 6 per cent of the total, while investments of Belgium-Luxembourg accounted for 1 per cent of the total." (*Foreign Investment in the Republic of South Africa*, U. N. publication by the Unit on Apartheid.) With West Germany and Italy added to the list of fingers in the pie, as well as Japan, it is clear that the affairs of South Africa now involve almost the whole of the capitalist metropolitan world.

Simultaneously, racism and capitalism in South Africa have not merely created conditions similar to colonialism within this country, but they have reached a stage where the economic and political forces look beyond the borders for new fields of exploitation. Recognising that the existence of stable, progressive, developing independent African states is a negation of the basis of apartheid, South Africa is not averse to influencing or directly interfering in the direction of these states. The alliance with Portugal and Southern Rhodesia against the African liberation movements, the annexation of South West Africa, the openly threatening attitude towards Zambia are indicative of the expansionist character of the racist republic.

The South African colonial and racist regime makes a mockery of the principles of the United Nations and all the international, cultural, political, economic and religious concepts of human rights, equality and dignity. Numerous decisions have been taken by the United Nations, by Afro-Asian solidarity and tricontinental movements and others, to impose economic, political, cultural, sporting and other forms of sanctions against the racist regime. Many governments and millions of people have to their credit responded to these resolutions. These have been major and important victories for our cause. However, a vast amount is still to be done, especially in Britain, Western Europe and the United States, to bring the international community to the realisation that the struggle against apartheid involves all who uphold the principles of humanity, justice and progress.

It is hoped that this volume will contribute toward a better understanding of what it means to live under apartheid; and that it will rally further support for the heroic South African people who have once again launched an armed struggle for liberation.

All of the contributors to this collection of articles are South Africans. They have participated in the struggle against apartheid in one way or another, and continue to do so. Most of them have suffered the brutalities and indignities of the apartheid police state. They now live in exile from their homeland.

ALEX LA GUMA

London, November 1970

O. R. TAMBO: Born 1917, in Pondoland, South Africa, graduated in physics and mathematics, Fort Hare University College, Cape, 1941. In 1944, he founded the African National Congress Youth League; 1948, studied law and formed first African law partnership with Nelson Mandela, 1951. He was accused in Treason Trial, 1956; and left South Africa in 1960 on instructions of A.N.C. to organise international solidarity for the liberation struggle. At present, Mr. Tambo is Acting President-General of the A.N.C., stationed in Zambia.

CALL TO REVOLUTION

For centuries the White oppressors of our country have lived by the sword. Now they shall perish by the sword. For decades White supremacy has been maintained by the gun. Now freedom shall be achieved by means of the gun. Our aims are clear. There can be no turning back. The sound of gunfire has been heard from the banks of the Zambesi river. Very soon the sounds shall be heard inside the Republic itself. The tide of revolution will grow and develop until it covers the whole of Southern Africa. There can be no compromise with the fascists. Our struggle will not cease until apartheid and oppression have been smashed and freedom comes to all the people of South Africa.

The long struggle for freedom in our country has entered a vital new phase. Fully conscious of its responsibilities our national organisation, the African National Congress, has decided to call on all the African people and their allies of other races to take up arms against the hated apartheid regime which oppresses and exploits our people.

We have not embarked on our present struggle lightly. We know that the revolution in South Africa will be a long and bitter one calling for maximum sacrifices from all lovers of freedom. Yet our national organisation with full support of the vast majority of the nation has chosen this path as essential if we are to lead our country out of the nightmare of White oppression.

The founders of our nation – Seme, Makgatho, Montsioa, Mangena, Mapikela, Plaatje, Dube* and others – taught us that the African people were conquered because the Europeans had the guns and were better organised. In addition, our forefathers fought separately and divided. In this way the Whites were able to defeat our peoples one by one. Therefore we had to concentrate first on removing the divisions among ourselves and creating a single African nation.

Our people fought in many different ways against oppression and for freedom.

The White government of South Africa treated all the demands and struggles of our people with contempt, because they had armed might on their side. All peaceful methods of drawing attention to our grievances were ruthlessly abolished. The methods used to crush the national strike of May 1961 in protest against Verwoerd's White republic showed that the White minority was determined to maintain itself in power by force.

* Founders of the national movement

It was then clear that the African and other oppressed people could not hope to achieve their freedom except by organising their own liberation army and arming the masses to fight a revolutionary war of liberation.

The African Revolution which began after the Second World War reached its climax in 1960 when the largest number of African states achieved their independence. This process has continued, until today there are thirty-eight independent African states. Only the Southern part of our great continent still remains under foreign or White minority rule.

The elimination of foreign rule over the larger part of the continent of Africa has changed the balance of power in favour of the oppressed people. Despite the difficulties faced by the independent states as a result of the legacy of colonial oppression, they are doing their best to assist the freedom of the remaining colonies and foreign-ruled territories in Africa. In preparation for armed struggle we have received and will continue to receive the support of our brothers in the Free African states.

Except for a small number of traitors who are prepared to sell their souls for a mess of pottage, Africa will help us to free ourselves. Today the African drums of freedom are beating their message right inside the White-ruled countries of Southern Africa. The day of reckoning for White supremacy has arrived.

The structure of the apartheid state with its elaborate mechanism of security laws depends in the final analysis on the army and security forces for its continued existence. Supporting these armed forces is an administrative machine of civil servants and officials who carry out the numerous attacks on our freedom in the pass offices, Bantu Affairs offices, law courts, public and private jails, in town, country and farm. Our armed struggle will be directed clearly and specifically at all those who support, work with, and cooperate with the fascists in the oppression of our people. This includes all those business interests that help the apartheid armies and their police by producing weapons and materials of war. All the enemies of the people will not escape punishment.

All those, whatever their race, who dissociate themselves from the instruments of oppression and either refuse to help the government or remain neutral, will not be regarded as enemies of the freedom struggle.

The African people are the most oppressed and exploited people in South Africa. They are the basis of our struggle for freedom and the most reliable force in our liberation movement.

But they are by no means alone in the struggle. The Indian people are today faced with complete economic ruin as a result of the Group Areas Act and other legislation. Like the African people they have no political rights whatsoever. The Coloured people similarly face, as they have done for many decades, racial humiliation and exploitation.

These people are part and parcel of the oppressed majority in our country, and their destiny is inseparable from that of the African people. Their place is alongside the freedom fighters against apartheid.

The enemy will do everything to divide and cause confusion among the oppressed with the help of the few traitors ready to sell themselves for money and favours from the oppressors. But our policy will be to secure unity in struggle among all oppressed people.

Also worthy of mention is the small group of Whites who have been prepared to turn their backs unreservedly on White privileges to fight side by side with the oppressed masses. Although they are few, such Whites are the salt of the earth and our armies will welcome the support of honest White supporters who have proved themselves in years of struggle against oppression.

It will require all our political skill and leadership to build a powerful movement of all revolutionary forces to support the armed struggles, based on unity, first of all, of the African people, and then of their allies among the Indian, Coloured and White lovers of freedom.

All those who hate apartheid and the system of racial oppression that has been practised in our country for so long, must work closely together under the leadership of the African National Congress in the armed revolution until victory is won.

Revolution calls for supreme vigilance, organisation and capacity to sacrifice. The movement needs men and women willing to fight and to perform all the tasks of war. In the political sphere we need organisers, propagandists and activists who will spread the message of struggle all over the country, in towns, rural areas and farms. Men and women, students workers, peasants, religious people – all must join the struggle and find a place in it.

Special responsibility in the revolution will rest on our splendid youth who have already shown that they are capable of great deeds. The armed struggle will require that our young men and women prepare themselves to learn the arts and skills of war and then fight with weapons in hand for freedom. This will be a great challenge to the youth, on whom the nation depends for victory in the revolution.

Our task is to organise and lead the struggle for freedom in South Africa. But we must not forget for a moment that Africans in other parts of Africa – in Mozambique, Zimbabwe, Angola, South West Africa, Guinea-Bissau – are engaged in the same struggle, confronting the same enemies. Therefore we are working closely with other freedom movements in the struggle against colonialism and White minority rule.

There is hardly anybody who can be found to support apartheid except those who profit by the exploitation that goes with it. All progressive mankind condemns and abhors apartheid.

The African states know that they cannot really be free until this monster has been eliminated from the continent. The Afro-Asian states at the United Nations and elsewhere have played a leading role in exposing the evils of apartheid and initiating measures to isolate the South African White rulers in the political, military, economic and social spheres.

All the Socialist countries actively support our cause. Millions of common people who hate oppression of others in the imperialist countries have always stood on our side in the struggle for freedom.

Even the big financial interests that are trading partners of South Africa in Japan, U.S.A., Britain, France and West Germany who benefit from our shameless exploitation are too ashamed to support apartheid openly. South Africa has become "leper of the world", and our planet will be a cleaner place after apartheid has been destroyed.

Now the task is to mobilise all the sympathy of the world into a mighty solidarity movement in support of the armed struggle in Southern Africa. The people of the world must be told why we have taken up arms and what we fight for. All the pressures that have hitherto been applied against South Africa must be greatly intensified. The White minority regimes must feel the indignation of the world at their continuing defiance of progressive opinion. Not only must the White supremacists be isolated but full material assistance must be afforded to the freedom fighters in the battlefield.

We do not imagine that the defeat of imperialism in Southern Africa will be quick or easy. We realise it will be long-drawn and bloody. But we are confident of the final outcome. As our forces drive deeper into the South, we have no doubt that they will be joined by the whole African nation: by the oppressed minorities, the Indian and Coloured people; and by an increasing number of White democrats.

The battle lines have been drawn up. There can be but one result: victory over the fascist oppressors and the establishment of a democratic state in South Africa!

VICTORY OR DEATH, WE SHALL WIN!!

BRIAN BUNTING: Born 1920, in Johannesburg; educated at Witwatersrand University; air mechanic and lieutenant in information service during World War II. In 1948, he was editor of the left weekly, *The Guardian*, and of *Advance* and *New Age* until banned in 1962. Member of Parliament as African representative in 1952, but expelled 1953 after being banned under Suppression of Communism Act. In 1962, he was banned again and placed under house-arrest. Mr. Bunting lives in London with his wife and family, working as journalist. He received an award from the International Organisation of Journalists, 1961. He is the author of *The Rise of the South African Reich* (Penguin Books).

THE ORIGINS OF APARTHEID

Apartheid means, literally, "apart-ness", the state of being apart, "separateness" or "separation", and in the South African context means racial distinction. According to the political correspondent of the Nationalist newspaper *Die Burger*, an Afrikaner writing under the pseudonym "Dawie", "the word was used for the first time in a leading article in *Die Burger* on 26 March 1943. In this reference was made to the 'Nationalists' policy of apartheid'. The next use of the term was again in a leading article in *Die Burger* on 9 September 1943, in which mention was made of 'the recognised Afrikaner standpoint of apartheid'. The first use of the term in Parliament, as far as I can determine, was on 25 January 1944 when Dr. Malan in his republican motion described the nature of the republic which he envisaged *inter alia* as follows: 'To ensure the safety of the white race and of Christian civilisation by the honest maintenance of the principles of apartheid and guardianship'."

Dawie said the word gained currency slowly, but "shortly after the war the word became generally used, especially because it was taken over untranslated into English political terminology. Naturally this created a stir. There is no reason why a translation, such as, e.g. 'separation' could not have been used, but the intention was most probably to suggest, by the use of a foreign word in the English language, something foreign and ominous, something so bad that there was no word at all in English for it!"

Dawie attributes the adoption of the word apartheid to some sort of hostile motivation by "the English", naturally regarded as unsympathetic to Afrikaner aspirations. But today apartheid has become an international word, like "Boer" and "trek", words which have been found to be untranslatable in most languages because they have a specific South African or Afrikaans connotation.

One further reason why "apartheid" has been found to be untranslatable is that it has no single specific meaning. In fact, to this day, there has been no agreement as to exactly what apartheid does mean. To Dr. Malan, who first used it, it obviously meant something which in the first place would preserve "the safety of the white race and of Christian civilisation". And it was by putting this principle first that the Nationalist Party persuaded the overwhelmingly White electorate to vote it into power in the 1948 elections.

The adumbration of the apartheid policy was the work of a special commission which had been appointed by the Nationalist Party and whose conclusions were embodied in a pamphlet issued by the Head Office of the Nationalist Party shortly before the end of 1947. It said:

"The policy of our country should encourage total apartheid as the ultimate goal of a natural process of separate development.

"It is the primary task and calling of the State to seek the welfare of South Africa, and to promote the happiness and well-being of its citizens, non-White as well as White. Realising that such a task can best be accomplished by preserving and safeguarding the White race, the Nationalist Party professes this as the fundamental guiding principle of its policy."

The pamphlet further declared that "the Bantu in the urban areas should be regarded as migratory citizens not entitled to political or social rights equal to those of the Whites. The process of detribalisation should be arrested."

The party proposed that apartheid should also be applied to the Coloureds, while the Indians were offered only the prospect of repatriation to India. At that time the party regarded the Indians as an unassimilable element in South Africa, and it was only in the time of Dr. Verwoerd that thanks largely to the refusal of the Indian Government to connive at it the repatriation policy was abandoned and the Indians accepted as a permanent part of the South African population.

Central to the idea of apartheid or separate development is the notion that the South African population is not and can never be an integrated whole, sharing a common citizenship. Dressing this up for international consumption, Nationalist Party leaders have stressed that separation is not the same thing as discrimination, and that every national group is entitled to the basic right of self-determination.

To Mr. Strijdom, who followed Dr. Malan as Prime Minister, "the purpose of the apartheid policy is that, by separating the races in every field in so far as it is practically possible, one can prevent clashes and friction between Whites and non-Whites. At the same time, in fairness to the non-Whites, they must be given the opportunity of developing in their own areas and in accordance with their own nature and abilities under the guardianship of the Whites; and, in so far as they develop in accordance with the systems which are best adapted to their nature and traditions, to govern themselves there and serve their community at all the various levels of their national life." (25 August 1955)

Mr. Strijdom's successor Dr. Verwoerd speaking in London in March 1961 described the apartheid policy as follows: "We want each of our population groups to control and govern itself as is the case with other nations. Then all can co-operate as in a Commonwealth – in an economic association with the Republic and with each other ... South Africa will proceed in all honesty and fairness to secure peace, prosperity and justice for all by means of political independence coupled with economic inter-dependence."

The present Premier Mr. Vorster likewise has said, "I believe in the policy of separate development, not only as a philosophy but also as the only practical solution in the interest of everyone to eliminate frictions, and to do justice to every population group as well as every individual. I say to the Coloured people, as well as to the Indians and the Bantu, that the policy of separate development is not a policy which rests upon jealousy, fear or hatred. It is not a denial of the human dignity of anyone, nor is it so intended. On the contrary, it gives the opportunity to every individual, within his own sphere, not only to be a man or woman in every sense, but it also creates the opportunity for them to develop and advance without restriction or frustration as circumstances justify, and in accordance with the demands of development achieved." (Broadcast speech on 14 September 1966, after being elected Premier in succession to the assassinated Dr. Verwoerd.)

Just how far these fine words are from the harsh reality of life in South Africa is by now obvious to most of mankind. Of South Africa's total population of 20 million (1970), only the 3.5 million with White skins have the right to vote for and be elected to the central Parliament which has legislative power over the whole country, including the so-called Bantustans. The 16.5 million Africans, Coloureds and Indians have no representation of any kind in any of the main law-making bodies of the country.

The fruits of the apartheid state also accrue mainly to the Whites. Of the total land area, only 13 per cent is allocated for the Bantustans or "homelands" of the African 70 per cent of the population. For the Coloureds and Indians there is not even the prospect of homelands, but only some sort of local self-government in ghetto enclaves within the White 87 per cent. Of the total national income, about 70 per cent is swallowed up by the Whites, who have possibly the highest standard of living in the world, though constituting only about 20 per cent of the population. It was estimated in 1968 that the average income among the Whites was more than ten times that of the other three races combined.

This is what apartheid is all about – a life of privilege and plenty for the Whites, based on the exploitation of cheap non-White labour. And the fact that this paradise can only be perpetuated on the basis of White domination is frankly admitted when Nationalist Party leaders speak in confidence to their own supporters. As Mr. Strijdom put it: "Our policy is that the Europeans must stand their ground and must remain *baas* in South Africa. If we reject the *herrenvolk* idea and the principle and the idea that the White man cannot remain *baas*, if the franchise is to be extended to the non-Europeans, and if the non-Europeans are given representation and the vote and the non-Europeans are developed on the same basis as the Europeans, how can the European remain *baas* .. Our view is that in every sphere the Europeans must retain the right to rule the country and to keep it a White man's country."

Premier Verwoerd, speaking in the House of Assembly on 25 January 1963 said: "Reduced to its simplest form the problem is nothing else than this: We want to keep South Africa White ... 'keeping it White' can only mean one thing, namely White domination, not 'leadership', not 'guidance', but 'control', 'supremacy'. If we are agreed that it is the desire of the people that the White man should be able to continue to protect himself by retaining White domination, we say that it can be achieved by separate development."

Speaking at a meeting in Durban on 13 March 1970, Premier Vorster, mindful that in an election campaign in which he was under pressure from the right-wing *verkramptes* he must put his cards on the table, said: "South African nationhood is for the Whites only. That is how I see it, that is how you see it, and that is how he will see it for the future."

His Deputy Minister of Bantu Administration, Dr. Koornhof, made it even clearer at an election meeting in Hopetown on 16 March 1970: "In White South Africa only the White man was *baas* and the Nationalist Party would maintain this position forever, with force if necessary."

The dilemma at the heart of Nationalist Party policy is that what they most need is at the same time what they most fear. They need Black labour to create White prosperity; but they fear the consequences of the integration of White and Black in a common society. With what longing did Premier Verwoerd speak when he addressed the Senate on 3 September 1948: "Nobody will deny that for the Native as well as for the European complete separation would have been the ideal if it had developed that way historically. If we had had here a white South Africa in the sense in which you have a white England and a white Holland and a white France, and if there had been a Native state somewhere for the Natives, and if this white state could have developed to a self-supporting condition, as those European states have developed by themselves, then we would certainly not have had the friction and the difficulties which we have today."

But, he said, it was not "within the realm of what is practical". The flow of Black labour must continue – yet the consequences of integration must be avoided. Thus ever since 1948 the Nationalist Government has steadily preached "separate development", while the economy has become more and more dependent on Black labour. The compromise on which the Nationalist Government is concentrating is to try as far as possible to convert all Black labour to migratory labour, to prevent the establishment of a permanently *settled* Black proletariat in the heart of a White-dominated society. This is the *raison d'être* of the policy of Bantustan, of homelands, of border industries, of the pass laws, of the Group Areas Act and the mass movement of non-White populations from one area to another. The myth of the creation of "a Native state somewhere for the Natives" has to be perpetuated as the only possible moral justification for the maintenance of White domination in the rest of the country – the so-called White South Africa where the riches of the Republic are concentrated.

This ambivalence in the White man's attitude towards the indigenous population can be traced back to the earliest days of White settlement in South Africa. Van Riebeeck and his party had been sent out to the Cape in 1652 with strict orders from the Dutch East India Company to keep the establishment as small as possible and to limit their perspectives to the setting up of a refreshment station which could victual ships passing by on the long voyage to India. There was no intention to found a permanent colony, or to embark on any programme of expansion. Indeed, the Company feared the consequences of overclose contact with the indigenous population, and at one stage seriously considered building a canal from Table Bay to False Bay so that the Cape Peninsula could be turned into an island and isolated from contact with the mainland and its peoples. The remnants of the famous hedge built by Van Riebeeck to mark the outer limits of the station are still to be seen in the botanical gardens at Kirstenbosch, Cape Town.

The hedge was only the first of many futile attempts to mark the boundary between White and Black South Africa. The Company had ordered Van Riebeeck to treat the Natives with friendliness and not to interfere with their affairs, but in his correspondence with the Directors Van Riebeeck sets down how easy it would be to deprive them of their cattle, and to press them into service as slaves. Though the Company formally rejected these proposals, it soon became evident that the Cape settlement had developed a momentum of its own independent of the Company's will. It was a mere five years before permission was given to some of the Company's servants to set up as independent colonists, and with this the mentality of the White supremacist was created.

"The presence of white settlers determined the composition of the new society at the Cape," writes M. F. Katzen in *The Oxford History of South Africa.* "Slaves were imported on a small scale from the beginning of the settlement, but became an important and permanent element in the new society, once private agriculture became established in the south-west Cape towards the end of the seventeenth century. The indigenous herding and hunting societies had largely disappeared as autonomous entities by the late eighteenth century. The Khoikhoi exchanged their sheep and cattle for European goods, white settlers occupied their grazing lands, smallpox and other epidemics caused great mortality; some groups retreated inland, others remained and their chiefs accepted VOC (Dutch East India Company) staffs of authority; many broke up altogether. The San, too, lost their hunting land and retreated with the game, but guerrilla warfare between settlers and the San on the Cape's northern fringes grew so intense after 1715 that the San were systematically exterminated. During the process of the displacement and destruction of the indigenous societies, many Khoikhoi and some San were incorporated into the new society as servile dependents of white farmers, working for barely more than their keep as herdsmen, domestic servants, or agricultural labourers. In the course of time cultural barriers between the various elements in Cape society broke down, partly as a result of widespread miscegenation between whites, slaves, Khoikhoi, and San, which foreshadowed the emergence of the Afrikaans-speaking Cape Coloured people."

Bushmen

At first the population barriers at the Cape were not based so much on race as on the difference between bond and free, between Christian and heathen. There were no laws forbidding racial intermarriage or sexual union, though while the latter was common, the former was rare, the most celebrated case being the marriage in 1664 of Eva, the baptised Khoikhoi woman who acted as the Company's interpreter, to Pieter van Meerhoff, explorer and surgeon. Nevertheless, the attitude of the White settlers towards the indigenous population (not to mention the slaves) was sufficiently unhealthy for Van Riebeeck's successor Wagenaar to issue an instruction in 1662: "The Hottentots and Capemans, with whom a free access has been hitherto allowed, shall still continue to enjoy the same; and you will on no account suffer them, out of wantonness, or upon trifling causes, to be called by the garrison, the cattle herds, or the sailors, 'black stinking dogs', still less to be kicked, pushed or beaten . . ."

According to historical account, the expression "black, stinking dogs" originated with Van Riebeeck himself. In his *History of South Africa*, Professor C. W. de Kiewiet says of the attitude of the colonists towards the locals:

"According to their belief it was more than their arms that made them prevail over the natives, and their superiority depended on more than their intelligence or their institutions. Their superiority was born of race and faith, a quality divinely given which could not be transmitted to other races or acquired by them. 'The black stinking dogs', as van Riebeeck already called them, suffered from an inferiority, predestined and irreparable, which fixed their place in a society of white men. Economically they had their place in the field and the kitchen; socially and politically they stood outside the circle of the rights and privileges of white men; even legally they existed in an ambiguous region between law and the arbitrary will of their masters."

"Their superiority was born of race and faith" – this has remained the fundamental tenet of the White supremacists from that day to this. And the Dutch Reformed Church, with its Calvinist fundamentalism and its emphasis on predestination and the writings of the Old Testament, was the spiritual rock on which this faith was founded. During the early years of White settlement, the Church was probably the strongest binding factor which held the community together and enabled it to maintain the unity and determination which was essential for survival. The Dutch Reformed Church was the Cape's State Church, and it was not until 1780 that freedom of worship was extended by law to any other church. It was the Dutch Reformed Church and the Bible which nourished the *trekboer* in his isolated wanderings. It is the Dutch Reformed Church which provides the spiritual justification for apartheid today, which assures its flocks that the laws of the state derive from God and are therefore beyond question. The marriage of the Dutch Reformed Church and the Nationalist Party is as close and enduring today as ever, each bolstering and supporting the other, ensuring the unity of the *volk* in the spiritual and temporal field.

When the British occupied the Cape for the second time in 1806, one hundred and fifty years of Dutch rule had left the colony with a population of 26,000 settlers, 30,000 slaves, and 20,000 "free" Coloureds in White employment. Contact had already been made between the colonists and the Bantu-speaking peoples of the central and eastern Cape, and this was to be greatly accelerated both by British rule and by Boer withdrawal from the British domain. The Afrikaner's struggle for apartheid was thereafter to be fought on two fronts, for he had to protect himself against two enemies – the Blacks and the English.

The colonists had always been resentful of authority, but they were doubly so when the authority was British. For the British were not only non-Afrikaners. They were also responsible for the abolition of the slave trade in 1807 and ultimately for the abolition of slavery in South Africa in 1834. The manifesto of the Trekker leader Retief, giving the reasons why his party intended to leave the Cape, whilst proclaiming "we will take care that no one is brought into a condition of slavery," at the same time declared: "We will establish such regulations as may suppress crime and preserve proper relations between master and servant ... We complain of the severe losses which we have been forced to sustain by the emancipation of our slaves, and the vexatious laws which have been enacted respecting them."

Whether or not the maintenance of slavery was the main issue, there is no doubt that the desire to re-establish "proper relations between master and servant" was the driving force which sent the majority of the Trekkers into the wilderness rather than continue under alien rule.

In his *History of South Africa* already quoted, Professor de Kiewiet says: "But it [the Trek] was pricked also by a deep sense of grievance. In ways both great and small very many innovations of the British Government had been offensive to the Dutch population. The western districts had suffered most from the depreciation of the Rix dollar and the emancipation of the slaves. Both eastern and western districts had resented the influence of Ordinance 50 (abolishing legal restrictions) upon Hottentot labour. There were few sections that did not feel that the effort of the British Government to apply the same law to all classes of the population cruelly upset the proper relationship between white and black, between master and servant. In the mouths of the Trekkers no grievance was more bitter than the refusal of the British Government to maintain 'proper relations between master and servant'."

Retief expressed the Trekkers' desire "to live in peace and friendly intercourse" with the native tribes, but Land-drost Andries Stockenstrom was of the opinion at the time "that the Boers are likely to reduce the natives to the conditions of the Hottentots lately", and in his book *Bantu, Boer and Briton*, published in 1929, the historian Macmillan adds: "His prophecy was only too accurate ... The Republics faithfully and rigidly adhered to the pre-1828 system which had entirely satisfied the old Boers, with the result that masses of the Bantu are now a proletariat, reduced to a condition not unlike that of the Hottentots a century ago."

And with prophetic insight Macmillan forecasts: "The forces of reaction still threaten to dominate the policy of the modern Union, sweeping back from the north with a vigour and a self-confidence born of the glorious achievements of the Great Trek."

The historian Eric Walker in his book on the *Great Trek*, mentions that the emancipation of the slaves "was all wrong in Boer eyes, wrong too in the eyes of many who were not Boers. Something must be done to get these people [the non-Whites] under control and save the economic and social foundations of the colony."

Walker mentions that the Boer women felt even more

strongly on the question of the emancipation of the slaves than their menfolk. "It was an outrage to that sense of racial superiority which was naturally stronger in the bearers of children than in the mere begetters of them. Ungodly, that was what it was"; and he quotes the complaint of the Trekker woman Anna Steenkamp in her diary that the British had placed their slaves "on an equal footing with Christians, contrary to the laws of God and the natural distinctions of race and religion, so that it was intolerable for any decent Christian to bow down beneath such a yoke; wherefore we withdrew in order thus to preserve our doctrines in purity."

The Boer Republics eventually set up by the Trekkers were based on constitutions which permitted of "no equality between coloured people and the white inhabitants, either in church or state". And as they were founded on land seized by force from the Africans, so they continued almost without change until they were destroyed by the British in the war of 1899–1902. The Boer President of the Transvaal, Paul Kruger, insisted as strenuously as Van Riebeeck or Retief might have done that "the black man had to be taught that he came second, that he belonged to the inferior class which must obey and learn" and that "severity was essential". It was the discovery of gold and diamonds which made the continuation of the isolation of the Boer Republics impossible, bringing about changes in the political and economic situation which necessitated unification and the concentration of productive forces, both human and material, for the mining and industrial revolution which followed.

It would be a mistake, however, to regard the effect of British rule in South Africa as wholly beneficent. Just as the Dutch settlers in the seventeenth and eighteenth centuries tended to ignore the principles laid down for them by the Dutch East India Company, so the British settlers in the Cape, absorbing the reactionary attitudes of the White community as a whole, forced modifications in the line desired by the Colonial Office. The origin of present-day pass laws and the masters and servants laws which have bedevilled race relations in South Africa are to be sought in British legislation of the nineteenth century. And whereas on the one hand the British may take the credit (or the blame) for the emancipation of the slaves, on the other hand they were responsible for the subjugation of the African tribes on the eastern frontier of the Cape and in Natal and the incorporation of their lands by conquest.

In their book *Class and Colour in South Africa 1850 to 1950* H. J. and R. E. Simons point out: "Few settlers in the Cape accepted the humanitarian's ideal of racial equality. Emancipation opened a new stage in the relations between white and Coloured; but it did not revolutionise the society or abolish discrimination ...

"Cape liberalism stood for racial tolerance. It was not a general characteristic of the white population. British immigrants rapidly absorbed the racial prejudices of the older white inhabitants, or acquired their own, as in Natal, where English-speaking settlers were dominant after 1850," and where they are still dominant today, though no more racially tolerant than the Afrikaners.

Each concession of self-government in South Africa resulted in an increase in White power and discrimination. The 1853 constitution was apparently colour blind, but by basing the franchise on income qualifications vested power firmly in the hands of the Whites who constituted the overwhelming majority of the electorate. The introduction of responsible government in 1872 saw an even firmer entrenchment of the White settler mentality, and it is no accident that even in the era when it was theoretically possible, no non-White was ever elected to membership of the Cape Parliament. The final concession of the British Government to the White supremacists was the passage of the Act of Union through the British Parliament in 1909, bringing into being in 1910 a state in which non-Whites were legally denied the right of election to Parliament and, in most of the country, the right to vote as well. The 1910 constitution, by entrenching White domination in the political sphere, inevitably paved the way for the final elimination of all vestiges of the non-White franchise, the victory of the minority Nationalist Government of 1948, and all the atrocities of the apartheid regime in the succeeding years.

Nor can the British working man escape his share of the blame. Brought out to South Africa after the discovery of gold and diamonds, he constituted the core of the artisan class for many decades. But while he must be conceded the merit for laying the foundations of the trade union movement, on the other hand he refused to share his skill with the non-White workers, and the formula he adopted, "the rate for the job" or "equal pay for equal work", though colour blind in principle, in practice effectively excluded non-Whites from the ranks of the skilled workers. The South African Labour Party, largely based on the English-speaking working class, was in its early years a firm supporter of the Nationalist Party demand for total territorial separation between Black and White. When the Labour Party joined the Nationalist Party in the coalition government of 1924, it helped to formulate legislation to extend and entrench the industrial colour bar, and supported General Hertzog in the first moves to deprive the African voters in the Cape of their common-roll franchise.

In *Class and Colour in South Africa* H. J. and R. E. Simons conclude their chapter on "The Liberal Cape" with the following words: "White working men fought against great capitalist combines for rights. The struggle rarely crossed the colour line to unite workers of all races in a common fight against the employing class. White workers usually chose to fight on their own, often under the banner of white supremacy. Racial discrimination, sponsored by governments, employers and white workers, divided the working class into antagonistic racial groups. As industrialism spread, the country moved ever farther away from the ideal state contemplated by Cape liberalism, in which all persons 'without distinction of class or colour should be united by one bond of loyalty and a common interest'."

The authors were writing of an earlier period in South African history, but it is equally true to say today that racial discrimination, sponsored by the government, employers and White workers, is dividing the working class into antagonistic racial groups.

Indeed, in its essence apartheid has always been a device for separating and dividing the peoples of South Africa in order to facilitate the domination and exploitation of the majority by the minority. In earlier days, separation could be achieved either by physical expulsion or voluntary withdrawal – the enemy could be driven across the Fish or Kei River, or the Boer could trek into the interior. Today total physical separation or isolation is impossible, for all twenty million of the South African people are enmeshed in the same economic system, ruled by the same parliament, compelled to live together, albeit in a state of hostile symbiosis. Yet in the name of apartheid the rulers of South Africa go through the same time-hallowed motions – "superfluous Bantu" (i.e. Africans who are unemployed, or too old or too young to work for the White man) are endorsed out of the towns and sent back to their "homelands". Not only is Black separated from White, but non-White is separated from non-White, Coloured from Indian – even the Africans are divided into ten separate ethnic groups each of whom are promised their own "homeland", complete with separate legislative assembly, national anthem and flag. Figures are juggled to show that the "White nation" is the largest single group of the South African population, as though this were adequate justification for their monopoly of political and economic power.

But there is apartheid even amongst Whites, and the Afrikaners withdraw from union with the English-speaking South Africans because only in isolation can they preserve the purity and supremacy of the *volk*. Laws have been passed to ensure that Afrikaner children are separated from English-speaking children throughout their school years, and in later life practically every social institution, from boy scouts to chambers of commerce, is duplicated for the Afrikaans and English-speaking sections. The Nationalist Party and Government, the civil service and state corporations, the police and permanent forces, are almost exclusively Afrikaans.

History has shown, however, that the isolationism of the Afrikaner is not inconsistent with expansionism. The small settlement which was once intended to be confined to the Cape Peninsula (6,000 acres inside Van Riebeeck's hedge) has grown over the succeeding years to incorporate not only the 472,359 square miles of South Africa itself, but also the 318,099 square miles of South West Africa. Today, in defence of "white civilisation", South African forces are deployed in Rhodesia, Angola and Mozambique, South African planes overfly the territory of Tanzania on reconnaissance missions, South African espionage groups operate in the capital of every independent African country, and South African Premier Vorster boasts that "nothing is going to prevent us from becoming the leaders of Africa in every field."

Apartheid is no longer (if it ever was) a domestic South African issue, but is threatening to overspill its borders and engulf the whole of independent Africa. In this ambition it is aided and abetted by leading Western powers like Britain and the United States who, while condemning racial discrimination in words, in practice bolster the apartheid regime with investments totalling £2,000 million (or about $4,840 million) which give them a higher return than they receive anywhere else in the world. And in the wake of the investments go political and military aid justified as necessary to help South Africa withstand the pressures of "international Communism".

Zambian President Kaunda himself stated as long ago as 1967: "Apartheid is on the offensive. The old commando spirit in South Africa is being implemented to extend the boundaries of the influence of apartheid. The Boer trek is still on and is now instrumental to the wider concepts of neo-colonialism, the pillar on which the minority regimes find their livelihood and derive their confidence."

Apartheid is not only destructive of the unity of the peoples of South Africa, but is now patently one of the most divisive agencies in a bitterly divided world. While apartheid rules, there can be no peace in Africa – perhaps not in the whole wide world. It is time to call a halt.

ARTHUR NORTJE: (1942–1970), graduated from Belleville (Western Cape) "Coloured" University College and taught in Port Elizabeth for one year. He studied at Jesus College, Oxford where he received his B. A. and Ph. B. Arthur Nortje died suddenly December, 1970. His poems have been included in anthologies and he was a prize winner in the Mbari (Nigeria) Poetry Competition. His collected works are now in preparation in London.

SCENE NEAR AN ETHNIC COLLEGE

Gull swerves and screams sharp doubt.
The wild grass curves
back from asphalt road. The ten-ton trucks
one spraying stone the other straw
roar on. The towering red-brick buildings
assault my sight with ranks of tall blind windows
split along the glass by spying sunbeams.

Lawns continue the narrative,
scornful in their crewcuts, trimmed
by some hangdog hottentot.
You hear repeatedly
the trains that chug away through thickets.
Aircraft in formation, swooping higher,
possess the gift of flight, can master peril . . .

The jets drill distance brittle, the executives
(nordic, incompatible with me)
stare sedately from a ninth-floor office.
Under the arches I bow through the shadows;
a shrill bird in the air asks of the sun
o where is the sea now, o where is home?

Cape Town 1964

HILDA BERNSTEIN: Born 1915 in London; South African by residence in Johannesburg for thirty years. She was the first Communist Party candidate elected to Johannesburg City Council by an all-White vote (1943-46). Founder member of Federation of South African Women and secretary of South African Peace Council. In 1960, she was detained under the Emergency Regulations after the Sharpeville massacre. She left South Africa in 1964 and now lives in London with her husband and four children. Mrs. Bernstein works as journalist and artist and is the author of *The World That Was Ours* (Heinemann, London).

SCHOOLS FOR SERVITUDE

How education in South Africa is being perverted to create bondage in a racial setting.

Education is the generator, the key. Without it life is restricted, the world remains closed. Today's world requires a highly developed system of education for the mastery of technology, for comprehension of the life around us, for participation. The advanced, industrialised countries are constantly expanding their education services, particularly university and higher technological education without which their manpower becomes obsolete.

In Bantu Education, South Africa has devised a unique system, "the only education system in the world designed to restrict the productivity of its pupils in the national economy to lowly and subservient tasks, to render them non-competitive in that economy, to fix them in a tribal world . . ."[1]*

The methods of education in any country reflect the social and economic system, and respond to the needs arising from this. In South Africa, the method is not a haphazard one which has simply grown out of historical circumstance. It is an integral, a vital part of the grand apartheid design.

Although segregation and inequalities have always existed in the South African schools, the present system with its enormous racial disparities is not simply the result of a colonial-type pattern of the past. It is a system remoulded to suit the ideology of the present. There is no ideal of universal education, free and compulsory in the elementary stages, with higher education equally accessible to all on the basis of merit, as set out in the Universal Declaration of Human Rights. The aim of education "directed to the full development of the human personality and to the strengthening of respect for human rights and fundamental freedoms", the idea that every child is the inheritor of world culture to the full extent of mankind's present attainments, and should have access to this common cultural heritage – this aim, this idea, runs completely counter to the system imposed on the people of South Africa.

The system is one presenting entirely different methods and objectives for the different sections of the population. The separateness of educational facilities for Africans, Whites, Coloureds and Asians is achieved not simply through schools, but by separate administrative structures, segregated methods of finance, differences in syllabus and

* See notes at end of section.

by different levels of achievement deliberately imposed to fit in with different expectations in employment. "Ultimately education is geared for the effective preparation of the Africans for their future occupations as unskilled labourers. Higher training is intended only for the small number of persons who can be employed in skilled works in African 'homelands' or African 'development schemes'."[2]

The Aims Decide the Conditions

The application of apartheid policies to education began seriously in 1953 with the passing of the Bantu Education Act. The Act removed education for Africans from provincial and rather haphazard control and handed it to the Ministry of Bantu Affairs. The Minister – at that time, Dr. Verwoerd, who later became Prime Minister – became the arbiter of education for all Africans, and he was quite explicit.

He spoke of the "wrong type of education" for Natives which created a frustrated people with "expectations in life which circumstances in South Africa do not allow to be fulfilled", and people who are trained "for professions not open to them". "Above all, good racial relations cannot exist when the education is given under the control of people who create wrong expectations on the part of the Native himself, if such people believe in a policy of equality, if, let me say, for example, a Communist gives this training to the Natives. Such a person will by the very nature of the education he gives, both as regards the content of that education and as regards its spirit, create expectations in the minds of the Bantu which clash with the possibilities of this country. It is therefore necessary that Native education should be controlled in such a way that it should be in accord with the policy of the state." He added grimly: "I just want to remind honourable members that if the Native in South Africa today in any kind of school in existence is being taught to expect that he will live his adult life under a policy of equal rights, he is making a big mistake."

Education *for* Natives, he later told the Senate, must be transformed into *Bantu* education ... "A Bantu pupil must obtain knowledge, skills and attitudes which will be useful and advantageous to him and at the same time beneficial to his community ... The school must equip him to meet the demands which the economic life of South Africa will impose on him ... There is no place for him in the European community above the level of certain forms of labour ... For that reason it is of no avail for him to receive a training which has as its aim absorption in the European community." He must not be subject to a school system "which drew him away from his own community and misled him by showing him the green pastures of European society in which he is not allowed to graze."

Mr. J. N. le Roux, later to become Minister of Agriculture, asked, "Who will do the manual labour if you give the Natives an academic education? I am in thorough agreement with the view that we should so conduct our schools that the Native who attends those schools will know that to a great extent he must be the labourer in the country."

"What is the use of teaching the Bantu child mathematics when it cannot use it in practice? ... That is quite absurd," said Dr. Verwoerd, an uncanny echo of a Nazi Minister laying down principles of education in Hitler Germany: "Why should girls bother with higher mathematics, or art, or drama, or literature? They could have babies without that sort of knowledge."[3]

The references to the "European community" in which there is no place for the Black man above the level of certain forms of labour, and to the green pastures of European society in which the Black man is not allowed to graze – (a splendidly revealing phrase – it could never be applied to a White man, who might loll in green pastures, but certainly would not *graze*) – might create the impression that there is actually a White community in South Africa which is separate from other races. The realities are that about two-thirds of the total African population lives in the so-called White areas, within the "European community", and there is not a single district, town or village in South Africa where the Whites are the majority. Nor does the Government consider this to be a violation of apartheid principles, because Africans "are only supplying a commodity, the commodity of labour ... It is labour we are importing, and not labourers as individuals ... Numbers make no difference."[4]

The Drop-outs

Education is compulsory for White children between the ages of 7 and 16 years. Compulsory education means that potential drop-outs are kept on at school until they are 16 years of age.

For Coloureds and Asians, education is compulsory between the ages of 7 and 14 "where there is a demand for it and accommodation permits." An estimated 73.5 per cent of Coloured children between the ages of 6 and 18 years were enrolled in schools in 1967, 89.19 per cent in primary schools, 10.81 per cent in secondary schools. No figures are available as to the potential Indian school population, but all Indian children in Natal and the Transvaal who reached the required age and applied for admission were accepted[5] – 77 per cent were in primary schools, 23 per cent in secondary schools.

There is no compulsory education for African children, who do not start school before the age of 8 years. According to the Minister of Bantu Affairs, about 78 per cent of African children of school-going age were attending school in 1968. The figure is misleading because of the high drop-out rate. Two out of three African pupils spend less than five years in school. The *Bantu Educational Journal* (a government publication) gave a total of 2,397,152 African children in school in June 1968, of whom 95.5 per cent were in primary schools, 4.12 per cent in secondary schools, and 0.38 in vocational and technical training schools. More than 70 per cent of the children were in the first four years of schooling. Most, in fact, leave school after (or before) completing the first four years. Many leave in the first year, many others in the second or third. And the position is not improving. In 1954, 70.94 per cent of all African children in school were in the first four classes. Fourteen years later the position is exactly the same.

Look at these figures:

Year	Primary School Enrolment		High School Enrolment	
1963	Sub A*	443,030	Form 1	20,800
1964	Sub B	332,390	Form 2	15,000
1965	Std 1	300,733	Form 3	10,000
1966	Std 2	239,141	Form 4	3,000
1967	Std 3	197,853	Form 5	1,800

A government commission (the Eiselen Commission on Native Education, 1949–1951) was of the opinion that "a Bantu child who does not complete at least Standard 2 has benefited so little that the money spent on his education is virtually lost."

What is the reason for this enormously high "drop-out" rate? There are many – lack of money, inadequate classrooms, gross overcrowding and double session schools, and the fixing of a number of "academic ceilings" for

* In White, Coloured and Asian schools there are seven primary grades, beginning with Sub-standard A; Sub-standard B, then Standards 1, 2, 3, 4; 5. The next stage is high school; Standards 6 to 10, sometimes called Form 1 to 5. For African children there is an extra year of primary school; Standard 6; and high school starts with Form 1.

African children, beyond which they are not permitted to go.

The fixing of "ceilings" was explained by Mr. M. Prozesky, Regional Director of Bantu Education in the Southern Transvaal. The first ceiling is Standard 2, when pupils who are not "mature enough or gifted enough to derive further benefit from academic studies" are simply debarred from further schooling. In Standard 6 there is another ceiling. Here students receive either a continuation certificate or a leaving certificate. To proceed to secondary school, the student needs a 50 per cent pass in the Standard 6 examination; those with an aggregate of between 40 and 49 per cent are given a school leaving certificate. Anything from 35 to 40 per cent of students cannot continue, stated the Education Director. "We eliminate them. They have reached their ceiling and can no longer benefit from schooling." He added that the system is not used in White schools.

In Form 3 (of high school) when the children write for their Junior Certificate examination, another ceiling is reached. Here pupils who "just scraped through", as well as those who had failed the exam, are not allowed to continue because "they are unlikely to matriculate".

So part of the phenominally high drop-out rate in African schools is accounted for not by "drop-outs" but by deliberate weeding out, elimination.

Finance

The total allocation to Bantu Education for the financial year 1969-70 was R39,280,000.* This is less than 0.4 per cent of South Africa's gross national product of about R10,000 million. South Africa spends about 4.5 per cent of its national income on education and training at all levels.

Fuller figures are available for 1965, when the gross

* 1 Rand = $1.30 or 58½ new pence (sterling).

national product was R7,255 million, with a figure of R326 million for education. Of this:

R252 million was spent on Whites .... 77 per cent
R31 million on Coloureds .... 9 per cent
R14 million on Asians .... 4 per cent
R29 million on Africans .... 8.9 per cent

These figures can only be understood in relation to the population figures. Per head of population, this was R74 for each White child, R17 for each Coloured child, R26 for the Asian child, and for Africans, R2.39.

National income of the White population per head is over ten times that of the other three races combined.

Education for Whites, Coloureds and Indians is paid for out of general revenue, the amounts being determined annually by parliament. Education for White children is a right, given to them free, with buildings, teachers, equipment, textbooks and writing materials.

African education is financed in two ways: an annual contribution to African education is made from general revenue, "pegged" in 1953 at R13 million (at that time, £6.5 million); to this is added the revenue from African general tax and miscellaneous receipts (boarding fees, etc.).

Africans contribute very large sums of money towards the cost of education in addition to the sums paid in taxation. They must pay for all their own books, except lower primary school readers, for all stationery, for handwork materials, school and examination fees, and of course, for uniforms, transport and lunches. Because the Bantu Education Fund does not have the money, African school boards and parents raise money to pay additional teachers' salaries. In 1967, a fifth of all African teachers were privately paid.

School boards have also had to raise half the cost of erecting schools for classes from higher primary up, and must pay for their maintenance. It was estimated that in 1965–66 African parents would have to pay at least

R17.25 a year to keep a child in lower primary school, R28 to keep him in higher primary, R48 in junior high school and R65 in senior high school.[6] But in November 1969, the Johannesburg *Star* published a report that the cost of education in schools in Soweto (Johannesburg) had risen an estimated 50 per cent in two years.

Again, figures by themselves do not necessarily reveal the true human story. R65 a year, or even R100 a year as it probably is today, would be a small amount for a White parent to pay to keep a child in high school. But the White parents do not have to pay – it is the Africans who pay. A Johannesburg municipal study in 1967 showed that 68 per cent of the African families in the city (which is the highest income centre in South Africa) had incomes below R53 monthly, which was the absolute minimum calculated for healthy living. In 1968 the revised budget for a family of five had risen to R59.70. (Note this minimum budget allows nothing for funiture, household goods, reading and writing materials, beer, cigarettes, recreation, savings, personal care, and so on. "The proportion who live below the breadline would be higher than this because Africans do, of course, spend money on items that are not included in poverty datum line studies. The effective minimum level of income is generally estimated at one-and-a-half times the poverty datum line figure, which would mean a family of six at Soweto should have at least R95.63 a month."[7])

Africans constitute 67.9 per cent of the population of South Africa, but their share of the nation's personal cash income is only 18.8 per cent. The Whites constitute 19.2 per cent of the population, yet receive 73.3 per cent of its income. According to these figures[8] the average income per head works out at R95 a month for Whites and R7 for Africans. The same survey estimated that *25 per cent of all urban African households had monthly incomes as low as between R1 and R19 a month;* 40 per cent had between R20 and R49; 20 per cent had between R50 and

R79; and only the remaining 15 per cent had family incomes of more than R80 a month.

A survey of 835 Indian households in Durban in 1969 found that between 50 and 60 per cent of the households had incomes below the minimum needed.[9]

"Several surveys among African school children revealed that 60 to 70 per cent were recognisably malnourished; 50 per cent needed nursing and medical attention, and almost 10 per cent required hospitalisation for diseases directly or indirectly attributable to malnutrition."[10]

The real, the constant, the terrible poverty of the mass of the African people, so often concealed beneath the veneer of prosperity, so carelessly dismissed by visitors who see a small proportion of Africans sharing the fringe-benefits of the booming economy – this daily struggle to survive, the child at school all day after a breakfast of black coffee, the child kept at home to care for younger children, the child without shoes or clothes to go to school, the child retarded by malnourishment, this is the reality which cannot be separated for one moment from education for African children. It remains an expensive luxury for most of them. Unable to surmount these terrible obstacles they slip back to the empty life of menial drudgery without hope of release, or make a choice between servitude and delinquency. They can scarcely be called "dropouts"; they are victims of apartheid.

The Burden on the Teacher

How is it possible to double the number of children attending school without a corresponding rise in expenditure? The Minister of Bantu Education has explained that it was done by:

1 The introduction of double sessions in the first standards.
2 Appointing women teachers for lower primary classes – they get paid less. The majority are teachers

with Standard 6 plus three years teacher-training, with a starting salary of £10.13.4 per month.

3 Re-grading of farm schools into junior and senior schools, with a corresponding saving on salaries since junior school teachers are paid a very small salary.

4 The conversion of funds previously allocated to school feeding to general educational facilities.

The school day in primary schools is divided into two sessions of three hours each. In double-session schools, two sets of children attend school, one for the first three hours, another for the second. In some schools, so acute is the overcrowding, that three sessions have been introduced.

The system of double sessions places an intolerable burden on teachers. It was introduced as a "temporary measure" with the introduction of the Bantu Education Act. But the *Bantu Education Journal* stated in April 1969, that there were 740,931 pupils in double sessions, mainly in the first two standards, and the total number had increased in a year by 5.1 per cent. Double sessions were operating at 51 per cent of the primary schools.

Double sessions also operated in 915 Coloured school classes, involving 30,295 pupils. The system is unknown in White schools.

The burden rests heavily upon child and teacher. Three hours schooling means that the rest of the day is spent roaming the township streets with nothing to do. But "it is not the function of the school to keep children off the streets or the veld by using well-paid teachers to supervise them," stated Dr. Verwoerd in 1954, and a later Minister of Education emphasised: "I want to put it very clearly that the keeping of children off the streets of our cities, the keeping of children away from the *tsotsi* gangs (juvenile delinquents), is not a function of education."

The teachers must repeat their morning teaching in the afternoon, using the same textbooks which cannot leave the classrooms. Double sessions have been used in the past in some developing countries in an attempt to achieve mass literacy, but the emphasis in these countries today is placed on higher education which is now put before the goal of universal primary education if for financial reasons these two are not compatible. In South Africa, incomparably the richest and most developed country of Africa, there need be no question of choice.

The depressed standard and status of the teachers is part of the Bantu Education scheme. "The Bantu teacher serves the Bantu community," declared Dr. Verwoerd, "and his salary must be fixed accordingly ... The salaries which European teachers enjoy are in no way a fit or permissible criterion for the salaries of Bantu teachers."

When the Eiselen Commission looked at African education in 1949, they found one teacher for every forty-two pupils. The latest report of the Bantu Education Department shows (outside the Transkei, and disregarding church and other private schools which receive no state subsidy) 1,806,653 pupils enrolled and 25,232 state-paid teachers – one teacher for every 72 pupils. "Faced with this scandalously inadequate official establishment, ill-fed families throughout South Africa cut down on the skim-milk powder and mealie meal and contribute cents saved to pay thousands of extra teachers privately, thus improving the teacher-pupil ratio to the still appalling 1:58.5."[11]

Not only the numbers of teachers are totally inadequate, but also the quality. In the 18 years between 1949 and 1967, enrolments in secondary and teacher-training courses had risen by 200 per cent. But the number of teachers for these classes increased by only 93 per cent, and the number of graduate teachers by only 21 per cent. So there were 52,000 additional students, and only 124 additional graduate teachers.[12]

The standard of training among African teachers has declined steadily since the Eiselen report found it to be unsatisfactory twenty years ago. At that time 18.6 per cent were without the qualification of matriculation. *Today the figure is 87 per cent.* In secondary schools only 53 per cent held lesser professional qualifications than the secondary schools' teachers' diploma.

Of the 31,597 White teachers in White schools in 1963, one in three held a university degree. Since 1928 all teacher-training for White students has been post-matriculation, and secondary school teachers are trained at universities.

The lowest qualification for which African teachers are now trained involves two years' professional training after the Junior Certificate, which is taken in Form 3 of high school (that is, two years before matriculation).

The highest salary scale for an African teacher is still lower than the lowest salary scale for a White teacher with equivalent qualifications. The ratios of salaries of African teachers to those of White teachers with the same qualifications were 41.9 per cent for men, and 37.9 per cent for women (in 1965).

The debasement of African teachers has turned them from professional people into instruments of apartheid. Teachers are public servants who can (and often are) dismissed without any reason being given. A long list of regulations govern their conduct; under "misconduct", thirteen possible offences are listed, including having an interview with the press, publishing letters or articles in any way critical of any State department or official, and being discourteous to any official. Many teachers have been dismissed on the suspicion that they are opposed to Bantu Education. Regimentation is part of the system; the teacher is a vital component, regimented and regimenting.

Their salaries are low enough, but on many occasions teachers have had to struggle to obtain them at all. The *Rand Daily Mail* reported in May 1969, that fifteen African school teachers in Thabu'Nchu had to send pleading letters to their creditors because they had not been paid yet that year. "We have written several letters to the Pretoria, but the Department of Education has not replied," stated a school board official. "Sometimes they take six months before paying the teachers. And it happens almost every year."

Farmers' Hands

At the very bottom of the teacher-scale are the teachers in farm schools. These are schools established by a White farmer on his property for the education of the children of his African employees. In 1968 there were 2,857 Bantu Farm Schools with 223,417 pupils and 4,557 teachers. They are all primary schools and the large majority are one-teacher lower primary schools, for stated government policy is to reduce farm schools to one-teacher, one-classroom units. There are no figures available of the numbers of African children living on White farms, but the schools may only be established if the owner of the farm wishes, and with the permission of the Department. There must be a minimum of twelve pupils and children wishing to attend must obtain the written permission of the farmer on whose land they live as well as the consent of the owner of the farm school, who may be a neighbouring farmer. The farm owner where the school is sited is the manager of the school and the teacher is his employee. The Department supplies the salaries; schools may close if there is a shortage of available funds.

The schools are built by the parents; as Dr. Verwoerd said, "Bantu mothers can erect walls where farmers allow it and the Department will provide windows, doors and roof. If the farmer withdraws his permission, these can be removed."

Women teachers for the schools are recruited locally to combat the danger of "unsuitable" teaching. The curricular includes "the basic idea of teaching the child in order to fit him for farm work."

"As regards the farm schools," said the Minister of Bantu Education in the Senate in June 1969, "we have made it compulsory that where the farmer wants these facilities, part of the school instruction ... must be training in the normal activities on the farm in order to encourage a feeling of industriousness on the part of those children, and particularly, to sharpen in their minds the fact that education does not mean that you must not work with your hands, but to point out to them specifically that manual labour on a farm is just as good a formulative and development level as any other subject is. In order to do this we create the opportunity so that if there is any farmer who has a farm school on his farm and who wishes to make use of the school children under the supervision of the teacher to assist with certain farm activities, this can be arranged in a proper manner to fit in with the curriculum and the plan of development which is envisaged or provided for that farm school."

In other words, the farmer who has the foresight to permit such a school is presented with free child labour for harvest and other occasions, under the supervision of the foreman-teacher, paid by the government!

"The pupil-teacher ratio which these figures indicate as well as the accent on manual training raise the question as to how far these schools are intended as educational institutions which can permit African children who attend them to proceed to higher education and move out of a dependence on European farms for a livelihood," comments the UNESCO report.

"It is to be hoped that farmers are not taking advantage of the permissive powers granted them to use the pupils to assist with farm activities, except in so far as one or two periods a week of practical instruction in farming methods may be of benefit to the children themselves," writes Muriel Horrell in *A Decade of Bantu Education*.

It is to be hoped ... "On one occasion," writes L. B. Tabata, "when a chief was to be installed, it fell to the children to lay a road so that the magistrate's car could reach the chief's place."

Under different conditions, it is a good thing for students in town or country to do some manual work, including farm work. If this were so for all students in South Africa, there would be no objection. Some time ago White university students at Stellenbosch announced they were going to do without servants. They made their own beds and swept their rooms for a whole week; then the experiment was declared a failure. Back came the Black servant, product of a school system that had trained him to meet the "demands which the economic life of South Africa imposes on him".

The Language Medium

The right to mother-tongue instruction – that children should be taught through the medium of their own native language – is supported by educationists throughout the world. In South Africa this inherently progressive principle is twisted to serve racist ends.

Nothing has caused more unhappiness to Africans in the field of education than the enforced introduction of education in the vernacular. There are two official languages in South Africa, English and Afrikaans. The Bantu languages are not used as a medium in government, industry, commerce or finance. They still lack a terminology to describe modern scientific concepts and their numerical systems are clumsy and difficult to use. These are, however, objections which a language must overcome if it is to survive in modern society.

The basic objection is that mother-tongue instruction is simply one more way of isolating Africans from the mainstream of South African life. It is yet another way of imposing a return to tribal and backward patterns. Unless Africans can speak a European language, preferably English, the doors of progress remain closed.

Africans feel that mother-tongue instruction has the effect of cramping them intellectually within the narrow bounds of tribal society and diminishing the opportunity of intercommunication between the African groups themselves and the larger world. They cannot escape the consequences of living in a technological age, and education through the limited vernacular cannot prepare them for this. They need to have access to world literature. Particularly those living in the towns must have mastery of at least one of the official languages.

"The African desperately strives for unity and is strongly opposed to any tendency to division among his people. The multiplicity of African languages has always been regarded as an impediment to unity ... to him, then, the re-tribalisation of schools and the emphasis it lays on the different vernaculars is a retrogressive step."[13]

Prior to the Bantu Education Act, mother-tongue instruction was used only in the first four or five years of schooling. Today all teaching up to and including Standard 6 is done through the vernacular and the aim is to continue the process up to matriculation. In addition, Africans must learn the two official languages.

"In South Africa, the policy of apartheid has had recourse to the choice of the mother tongue as the main medium of instruction at primary level (beyond which the vast majority of African children do not pursue their studies) in order to reinforce the linguistic, social and cultural isolation of the African population within the country as well as from the world at large."[14]

In White schools, teaching is conducted through the medium of either English or Afrikaans, with the second language taught throughout school life. Parents may not choose the language-medium for their children, who must attend a school conducted in the language commonly used in his home. This has reinforced the trend of separateness in education and ensures that contacts between the English-speaking and Afrikaans-speaking children are reduced. In the past – before the Nationalists changed the laws – parents could choose the language-medium, and in addition, there were some dual-medium schools where teaching was conducted in both languages.

Textbooks and Syllabus

Black South African children have a different syllabus to Whites, Coloureds and Asians. Their textbooks may be different, too, although sometimes they are revised and condensed versions of those used in White schools.

In African primary schools the syllabus is: religious education, a Bantu language, English, Afrikaans, arithmetic, writing, music, arts and crafts, gardening and environmental studies. In the higher primary course, social studies take the place of environmental study; and nature study, tree planting, soil conservation, needlework (for girls) and woodwork and metal work (for boys).

In the first two years, the school day is divided into two sessions of three hours each, including a half-hour break. Of the weekly curriculum of 825 minutes:

religious instruction and health parades take up
205 minutes;
Afrikaans, English and the vernacular language take up
380 minutes;
arithmetic takes up 140 minutes;
writing and singing take up 100 minutes.

Thus roughly 25 per cent of the time is spent on religious instruction and health parades.

In the third and fourth year, the time is increased and the curriculum spread over 1,650 minutes:

religious instruction and health parades, (300 minutes)	18 per cent
the three languages	36 per cent
arithmetic	15 per cent
environmental studies	8 per cent
gardening, handicrafts, needlework, singing and writing, (420 minutes)	25 per cent

In the secondary schools the syllabus is expanded to include natural sciences, social studies, and two subjects chosen from Latin or German (or any other approved language), mathematics or general mathematics. The three languages and religious education, physical education, music and singing, feature on the syllabus as well as agriculture, woodwork, arts and crafts, homecraft, biblical studies. In the higher secondary course, the syllabuses do not differ from other South African schools.

"Race Studies" in White Schools

The subject "Race Studies" has been introduced into high schools for White children, an innovation parallel to *Rassenkunde* in the education of Nazi Germany. The emphasis in Race Studies is almost entirely on the rural and primitive tribalism of the Bushmen, Hottentots and Bantu. The only sections of the syllabus devoted to the urban African reads as follows:

1 Administration and control.
2 Native locations and Native towns.
3 Compounds and hostels and bachelor Natives.
4 Problems: housing, indolence, juvenile crime, other forms of crime and deterioration of tribal authority.

Under the first heading, "Administration and care of the Bantu", the White student is taught that arrangements are made for "separation, reserves and guardianship" on the one hand, and for "employment of the Bantu by the European". Types of employment are "agriculture, mining, industries and servants", all of which are subject to benign "control". The assumption is that the Bantu must be grateful for his servitude.

The whole course inculcates the doctrine that the White man has been placed in South Africa by God as guardian of the Black, and this must be carried out through apartheid.

The Indian community is assumed to be anti-African. "One of the ways that the Indians have concentrated on in order to escape the Bantu danger is sending their children to schools in large numbers so that they may qualify themselves for other and better work." A section deals with "Attempts to Repatriate Indians" and infers that South African Indians are not South African but foreigners. Anti-Indian prejudice on the part of Whites is said to be "understandable."

Antagonism between Africans and Coloureds is suggested by one section of the textbook dealing with Africans in the Western Cape, who, according to the book, have upset the economy of an area which once employed only Coloured labour. The Coloureds are said to be strongly opposed to the entry of the Bantu into their field of employment and into their residential areas.

The textbook exhorts that "vigilance must be maintained against the evil practices of wicked people scheming to exploit Bantu ignorance for the sake of financial gain, and against the spreading of foreign ideologies about which they have no clear notions."

The idea of apartheid, called "territorial separation" and "territorial segregation", is implanted as being inherent in South Africa from the very beginning of contact between Black and White.

History textbooks show how God leads a nation to pious deeds and how a Divine plan with a nation is carved out ... The idea of a chosen people is found in many textbooks. The hand of God reveals itself in the history of the Afrikaner in South Africa. They had been planted by God as a new nation on the southern tip of Africa and had been wonderfully preserved from being wiped out.

A Standard 8 guidance book underlines the differences that are presumed to exist between Whites and non-Whites: "The point of view of certain foreign clergymen that Whites and non-Whites should inter-marry and that, in the name of Christianity, is too incisive a change in the culture pattern of the non-White and the White. Such a thing can only create confusion and degeneration. All things considered the coming about and continued existence of the White Christian civilisation in spite of the mass of non-Whites can be seen as nothing less than a disposition of the Almighty."

The myths that the Dutch landed in South Africa in an empty territory, and that the early settlements of Whites were marked by massacres of innocent unsuspecting Whites by the Africans, are inculcated into the child's mind. The majority of Whites in South Africa believe that White settlers three hundred years ago arrived before any native tribes, who appeared later on the scene. Land tenure and its relationship to frontier clashes between the Whites and Africans was one of the key aspects of early South African history. But as taught in the schools, the Africans were thieves, marauders and murderers, the White farmers blameless. So Bantu Education and White supremacy, like two sides of one coin, establish the inviolability of apartheid in South Africa. In a chapter on race relations in an official textbook this extraordinary statement appears: "In some countries where Whites settled, they soon inter-married with the non-Whites and a bastard population originated. In South Africa this did not happen." As though 1.5 million Coloured people do not exist. Yet the "founding father" himself, Jan van Riebeeck, married a non-White woman!

Further on, the book states: "Inter-racial residence and inter-marriage are not only a disgrace but are also forbidden by law. It is, however, not only the skin of the White South African that differs from that of the non-White. The White stands on a much higher plane of civilisation and is more developed. Whites must so live, learn and work that we shall not sink to the cultural level of the non-Whites. Only thus can the government of our country remain in the hands of the Whites.[2]

"As far as the higher primary and post-primary schools are concerned, it is the intention to give preference to the Bantu areas because this is in the first place where the Bantu development must be promoted generally. You may perhaps tell me that there is a great desire in the urban areas for post-primary schools in order to keep the children off the streets; that they should be brought into the schools rather than be allowed to remain on the streets where they become *tsotsis* and so forth. I want to put it very clearly that the keeping of the children off the streets of our cities is not a function of education ... For this reason it is our policy to restrict higher primary, but particularly post-primary, education in the urban locations, but not in the Native areas." – The Minister of Bantu Education, in the Senate, 15 May 1959.

The extreme shortage of secondary schools for Africans has been aggravated in recent years by the determination of the Government that high schools should be located in the "homelands". Children may live with their parents in the urban townships and attend primary school, but if they wish to take their education further, then they must be sent away to boarding schools in distant reserves. When the Department of Bantu Education stated they would crack down on school principals in Soweto who had enrolled as many as seventy pupils in a class at the beginning of 1970, the Secretary for Bantu Education, Dr. H. J. van Zyl, referred to the reluctance of parents to send their children to secondary schools in the "homelands". He then went on to complain about children going to the Soweto schools, who were not entitled to go because their parents were not legally resident in Johannesburg. "It is common knowledge," he stated, "that Bantu people readily adopt children belonging to relatives and friends. They take them in and regard them as their own." The Department took precautions against the enrolment in the schools of such children, but "whether the precautions we take are foolproof or not I cannot say." The extraordinary gap between attitudes to White children and Black children is clearly revealed in this comment. To try and picture White children in South Africa facing a similar educational dilemma is quite impossible.

The problem confronting African parents in the towns is very great. Crime and delinquency in the townships is enormous. The hunger for education for their children forces some parents to send them away to schools in the reserves, rather than see them growing up in ignorance, idleness and danger on the streets of the townships. But they do not want to send the children away. Apart from the reluctance of any parent under normal circumstances to send young children far away to boarding schools, there are other factors. An official of the Bantu Education Department stated, "I think they're afraid their children won't be allowed back. They think a bursary to a school in the homelands will be an obstacle to their return."[15] Africans, even minors, may so easily lose their tenuous rights to live in urban areas.

Then the bursaries for boarding schools do not cover the cost of travel and of clothing, and only part of the cost of books. Some bursaries go as high as R100 annually. Not much more than R100,000 a year is allocated for these at present. It seems as though even the "homelands" schools have not room for all who wish to study. "A survey of the sprawling North Sotho homeland in the Transvaal has shown that instead of finding educational facilities 'in abundance', hundreds of pupils were turned away when high schools there opened last month," the *Star* reported on 21 February 1970. The reason: inadequate classrooms and boarding facilities. "Schools, too, had to reject children who sought admission but had no relatives to stay with in neighbouring villages." The report referred to the "go to the homelands" advice given by the Department of Education earlier in the month. A reporter visited seventeen high schools in Middelburg, Sekukuniland, Zebediela, Pietersburg and Potgietersrus and found all but four were essentially day schools serving local communities and unable to take children from other areas. At a private Roman Catholic school only 56 out of 300 girls who applied for Form 1 could be taken (the Department limits the number of children a private school may take). Tshebela Secondary, a boarding school at Molepo Village in Pietersburg rejected 515 applications because the places were all filled.

The school year in South Africa begins in January. Each year brings a new quota of heartbreak for children shut out of the schools. In January 1970, newspapers carried many stories about the children of Soweto who were turned away because there was no room for them in the desperately overcrowded classrooms. The children arrived in neat uniforms – parents believe they are more readily accepted if they have a school uniform – many of them as early as six o'clock in the morning to be first in the queue. They crowded the school courtyards and thousands jammed the corridors. When school principals told them there was no room, some burst into tears and went home; others went on waiting hopefully, until the schools closed in the afternoon.

At one Orlando (Soweto) high school, more than 200 children sat in groups within the school grounds. They came every day for more than a week. "What hurts me is that there is nothing I can do for them," the headmaster said. "But they don't seem to understand that."

The schools tried to stretch to absorb more children, packing huge classes into every available space, even without enough teachers. A few days later an official said the Department would "crack down" on principals who had enrolled as many as 70 in a class. The regulations lay down a maximum of 55. They must go to the "homelands", the official said. More secondary schools will not be built in the townships, only in the reserves.

Soweto has an estimated population of three-quarters of a million, but nobody knows the number of school-age children who live there. Only 16 out of the 225 students in Soweto's high schools passed the matriculation examination in 1967.

The general decline in standards brought by Bantu Education has caused a corresponding drop in the percentage of children who matriculate. Of 825 African students in all South Africa who passed matriculation in 1965, only 322 obtained university entrance qualifications; and of these, only 172 had mathematics and 11 biology and physics as a subject.

In 1965, 50,000 White students wrote for matriculation. Of these, 20,714 failed; 12,234 obtained university passes, the balance obtained school leaving passes.

Vocational Training

Trade and vocational schools are situated mainly in rural areas. "I can only say that the intention is in the first place to concentrate vocational training mainly in the Bantu areas, in order to meet the need which exists for people with vocational training to assist in the development of the Bantu communities themselves," stated the Minister in parliament in 1959.

There are now 13 trade schools for African boys with an enrolment of 1,508. The picture is complicated by the fact that some secondary schools are now "technical" secondary schools, combining general studies with technical training. In 1968 there were over four hundred African girls doing vocational training in dressmaking and similar subjects.

Trainees who qualify are eligible for employment in African areas only. Access to trade and technical schools depends on a Standard 6 certificate, so the number of Africans eligible for the course is necessarily small. Africans have limited access to qualified jobs outside the reserves and African townships. The position is directly related to apartheid policy in skilled work, and the laws concerning job reservation.

In 1965 there were 20,719 Whites in departmental vocational schools, 6,172 full time in technical colleges, and 38,838 part time in technical colleges. (In the same year, there were 375 Africans in technical schools and 841 in trade schools.)

The Universities

"In America, Mr. Justice Hiemstra said, there were 225 new Negro graduates per 100,000 population. For the Bantu in South Africa there were 1.7 graduates per 100,000 in 1967." – *Rand Daily Mail*, 26 May 1969.

The introduction of the Extension of University Education Act in 1959 closed the doors of the universities to non-White students.

Until 1959 there were two "open universities" in South Africa, Cape Town and the Witwatersrand, which accepted non-White students and practised no academic segregation, although there was segregation of Whites and non-Whites in the sporting and social activities of the universities. In addition, the Fort Hare University in the Cape was also "open", although predominantly for African students. Its 1957 enrolment, a typical one, had 283 Africans, 48 Coloureds and 47 Indians, and occasionally there had been White students at Fort Hare.

The universities of Stellenbosch, Pretoria, the Orange Free State and the Potchefstroom University for Christian Higher Education, did not accept any non-White students, and the Rhodes University at Grahamstown only accepted non-Whites for certain post-graduate courses. The University of Natal accepted non-White students, but generally only in segregated classes.

In 1959 complete university apartheid was introduced. Enrolment at South African universities in June 1959, just before the introduction of university apartheid was: Whites, 35,095; Coloureds, 822; Asians, 1,516; Africans, 1,871. The majority of African students were at Fort Hare (319) with 187 at Natal; 1,252 were enrolled at the University of South Africa, which does correspondence courses only. There were 113 African students at Cape Town and Wits, the open universities. There were 461 Coloured students at Cape Town, 70 at Fort Hare, 50 at Natal and 211 at the University of South Africa. Of the Asian students, the majority were in Natal (489) and the University of South Africa (601), with 326 at the open universities.

This tiny number of non-White students mingling among the White students was regarded by the Government as a threat to apartheid. The 1959 Act established the principle of separate higher education for each group, while for the Africans, the group was again split into "ethnic" tribal divisions. A second Act, introduced simultaneously, converted Fort Hare from an open university into a tribal college for the Xhosa. Two new colleges were built, one to serve the Sotho group at Turfloop in the North Eastern Transvaal; Zulus are served by the University of Zululand at Ngoya in the Mtunzini district of Natal.

The University College at Durban was reserved for Indians, the University of the Western Cape for Coloureds and the Medical Faculty of the University of Natal for Indians, Coloureds and Africans. In accordance with the policy that "education should stand with both feet in the Reserves and have its roots in the spirit and being of Bantu society" the new colleges were built far from urban areas.

The Act made it a crime for Whites to attend non-White universities while non-Whites could only attend "White" universities if the course they wished to study could not be undertaken at the tribal colleges, and provided the Minister gave his permission. In 1965 of 145 applications made to the Minister for permission to study at "White" universities, 24 were granted. In 1969 there were only 2 African students at Cape Town, 5 at Wits, and 175 at Natal, of whom most were at the segregated Medical School. There were 774 Coloured students in the college at the Western Cape, 1,621 Asians at the Indian College in Natal, and Africans attending the tribal colleges were: 486 at Fort Hare, 428 in Zululand and 671 at Turfloop. Including those doing correspondence courses at the University of South Africa, there was a total of 1,598 Coloured students, 3,354 Asians, 3,911 Africans; there were 68,549 White students, of whom 16,557 were at the University of South Africa.

Fort Hare was taken over by the Government and converted into a Xhosa tribal college. Founded in 1916 with funds mainly provided by the churches, it had a fine academic tradition and had trained many African leaders; but now it did not "fit in with the plans for the development of the various national groups in South Africa as envisaged in the Extension of University Education Act and the Promotion of Bantu Self-Government Act."[16] The principal, Professor Z. K. Matthews was informed he would be reappointed if he resigned from the African National Congress; he refused to accept reappointment under this condition. Other members of the staff were not reappointed, or were retired, or resigned. Students protested and passed a resolution reaffirming their outright condemnation of university apartheid legislation. As a result of this, eleven students were not readmitted. Explaining the sackings and resignations of so many of the most prominent academicians at Fort Hare, the Minister of Bantu Education stated: "I disposed of their services because I will not permit a penny of any funds over which I have control to be paid to any persons who are known to be destroying the Government's policy of apartheid."

New regulations were passed to control the registration and behaviour of students. Each year, students at the ethnic colleges must apply for permission to report for registration, and with the application form must send a testimonial of good conduct by a minister of religion. Registration may not be refused without reasons being given. Students are not allowed to hold meetings or belong to student associations without permission, and they have been debarred by the Government from associating with the National Union of South African Students.* Ethnic college students enjoy none of the rights of students in other countries, nor even a measure of those still permitted to White students.

The staff as well as students are subject to stringent and humiliating restrictions. White members of the staff are employees of the college council (there are two councils, one White and one African, but the African council is purely advisory). Non-White members are civil servants, subject to all the restrictions of the civil service regulations plus additional curbs laid down in the disciplinary codes for the colleges.

There are substantial differences in pay between White and non-White members of staff – for example, the maximum salary for an African male professor at Fort Hare is less than the minimum salary for a White female professor, and the salaries paid to White personnel are much higher than those received by their non-White colleagues, irrespective of professional attainments. Although apartheid is supposed to provide opportunities for Africans to develop "in their own areas", at the end of 1969 nearly three-fourths of the lecturers at the three ethnic colleges which had been established ten years before to cater for the "special" cultural needs of African students, were White. The rectors of the three colleges (Fort Hare, Turfloop and Ngoya) are all White. For professors the ratio of White to Black is more than 10:1; for senior lecturers

* Students are not allowed to elect their own student governing bodies nor to affiliate with any national organisation.

it is more than 12:1. Only at the bottom rungs of the academic staff ladder – among the junior lecturers and "other teaching staff" do Africans outnumber Whites, but this category is an insignificant 15 out of 268. While student enrolment had increased three-fold in ten years – from 500 to 1,500 – and graduates from 50 to nearly 150, not all the students enrolled are properly qualified for university study, and not all are able to study for degrees. In 1963 only 322 of all students enrolled were taking degree courses, while 286 were taking diploma courses. And after ten years, there are still no medical and engineering faculties at the ethnic colleges. In 1968 and 1969 there were only 15 agricultural students and no graduates for those two years. There is a heavy concentration in arts and education, accounting for about two-thirds of the students (of whom one-fifth are 25 years of age or older). The Natal Medical School for non-Whites is producing seven or eight doctors a year.

"Neither enrolments nor degrees awarded, justify the statement that establishment of ethnic group colleges has provided increased university facilities for non-Whites."[17] (The number of graduates in 1956 was 144; in 1962 it was 105.) And the cost is very high. Dr. E. G. Malherbe, principal of the University of Natal, estimated that it cost the taxpayers about 13 times more to educate non-Whites at a tribal college than at the Natal University. In 1965 the cost per student was £1,000.

At the eight residential universities for White students, students' councils are elected by the students themselves and draw up their own constitutions. While White students are not controlled and treated like prisoners, as the students are at the ethnic colleges, even so the Security Police pay them a great deal of attention. In two months in 1968, an estimated sixty students were involved in police or government activity of one kind or another, according to the National Union of South African Students. White students active in N.U.S.A.S. had their passports withdrawn or refused; eleven White students reported that they had been approached by Security Police to act as spies on the campuses; twenty-one African students were expelled from Fort Hare for taking part in a protest against the installation of a new rector; seven more were being held in custody by the police before being brought to court on charges connected with unrest at the college. Quoting these and other accounts of student victimisation, the N.U.S.A.S. president said, "We are witnessing the largest and most intensive witchhunt ever carried on against South African students."

It is a constant assertion of the South African government that it is doing more for African education than any other country in Africa. A pamphlet issued by the Department of Information in 1965, *Education for Success,* claims: "In recent years the opportunities for university training for the Bantu have been considerably enhanced. So much so, that they are nowhere equalled in Africa." The pamphlet goes on to make the claim that standards in the African colleges "are identical to those of any other South African university." The Deputy Minister of Bantu Education, Mr. Blaar Coetzee, backed his claim that South Africa led all Africa in education by figures comparing the richest country in Africa with some of the poorest. Yet a former Director of Education in Natal, Dr. McConkey, said that hundreds of thousands benefited so little from schools that the expenditure on them was virtually wasted, and they were destined to forty or fifty years of unskilled work, poverty and ignorance. This, in a country so desperately short of skilled workers that this has slowed down the development of the economy, and skilled White workers are constantly being sought overseas.

A South Africa journalist, Anthony Delius, writing about advancement in Black Africa, suggested that "more sweeping in effect than even the coming of independence will be the eventual social changes brought about by the rapid expansion of education that is gathering momentum daily. Not long ago Black Africa could scarcely boast a couple of million school children. Now there are more than a dozen million and pretty soon there will be double this number.

"Kenya and Ghana between them, with a total population less than South Africa's, have about three million children at school, about equal in number to all the children at school in South Africa, African, White, Coloured and Asian.

"Once South Africa could claim that she had produced more African graduates (2,300) on her own soil than all of Black Africa put together and that she had the only university college catering for non-Whites (Fort Hare) in all the 3,000 miles from Sierra Leone to the Cape. Now the position has changed dramatically.

"A score of new universities has sprung up between the Sahara and the Zambesi. Nigeria has five universities where in 1960 she only had one. These universities between them have about 40,000 students today, and in the very near future will probably have 100,000. (Beyond the Sahara Egypt already has 100,000 students in her universities.) ... Uganda, population 7 million, has 2,500 students overseas, equal to South Africa's total non-White student population in institutions of higher education."

Zambia, five years after independence, has already put its colonial education record to shame. In 1964 Zambia had fewer than 9,000 children in secondary schools. In 1969 the figure was 35,000 and in 1970, 63,300 Zambians, of whom 2,000 are Whites. Zambia has a population one-third that of South Africa, but by 1968 it was spending twice as much as South Africa to educate its children.

In his paper *The Effect of the Policy of Apartheid on the Development of Science in South Africa*, prepared as part of a UNESCO survey, Professor E. H. S. Burhop, Professor of Physics in University College, London, wrote: "There are no registered non-White veterinarians, architects, civil, electrical or mechanical engineers. An African who qualified in civil engineering in 1962, has since left South Africa. One Indian has obtained high qualifications as a radio engineer." He wrote of the very low standard of equipment of the science laboratories in secondary schools for Africans, and quotes Dr. Birleys' figures: "In the African township of Johannesburg (with about 0.75 million Africans) there are four secondary schools which take children up to matriculation standard. I have recently surveyed their laboratories and equipment carefully. The schools have... between them thirteen Bunsen burners, six balances and three microscopes. They cannot possibly prepare their pupils for genuine university work."

Thou shalt not Teach Others

In South Africa today it is illegal for anyone to conduct a school or class which is "unregistered". Night schools and continuation classes fall under this provision. In White residential areas, schools or classes must not only register with the Bantu Education Department, but must also hold a permit from the Group Areas Board; there are a number of other conditions as well. "Registration" is granted where the Minister is satisfied that tuition will be in conformity with the general scheme of Bantu Education.

A former teacher, I. B. Tabata,[18] relates this story: "A retired African teacher of sixty, who had gathered a number of African children together, chiefly to keep them from the danger of the streets, was arrested and fined £75, or seven months. The magistrate when convicting him commented, 'You are a learned and respected man in the community, yet you keep on defying the law'."

The hunger for learning is very strong. Before the Bantu Education laws closed them down, there were many night schools held in garages in White areas where Black domestic servants who did not finish work until eight or nine at night, would come to study. And classes in small halls, rooms, even open spaces run by voluntary organisations, African and White, engaged in adult education.

If the claim of the Minister of Bantu Education in 1959 that an estimated 80 per cent of Africans in the 7 to 20 age group could be considered literate is correct, then adult education becomes a pressing problem. In 1963 the Minister gave 40 to 50 per cent as the general African literacy rate.

The high drop-out rate in both primary and secondary schools also makes the need for continuation of education very great.

The new laws had the effect of closing down most of the adult education schools and classes.

The principle that Africans should be mainly responsible for financing their education was made applicable to adult education as well as to primary, secondary and university education. In 1958-59, a sum of R46,000 was voted for grants to night schools and classes for Africans. In 1960 the amount was more than halved – R20,000. It was reduced to R2,000 in 1962-63, and halved again the following year. In 1965 the grants were discontinued. In addition to bearing the major cost of financing the expanding education for the children, Africans now have to bear the full cost of financing night schools and continuation classes for adults.

The Minister of Bantu Education also announced that he was "opposed to the existence of a large number of night schools in our White urban residential areas". This meant an end to night schools in areas where Africans work and live. Many night schools in White suburbs in all the large towns have been forced to close down.

UNESCO's report on the effects of apartheid in education summarises its findings as follows:

"The South Africa case in African education may be briefly stated as:

1 South Africa is rapidly expanding African education.
2 Africans are being trained to 'take over' in the 'Bantu homelands'.
3 Separate development, in education as in every other sphere, promotes rather than hinders good race relations.

"There is no doubt that African education has expanded at the primary level and that Africans themselves have financed this expansion. At secondary and university levels, the situation is different. Here African education has remained almost stationary. That Africans are being trained to 'take over' in the reserves cannot be supported either by the numbers who graduate, and so can hold official positions afterwards, nor by the degree of administrative responsibility which is at present permitted to them. That they are not being trained to play their part in a total South African society is explicitly stated by the South African Government itself. A key question in modern industrialized states is the number of nationals who are being trained for high-level scientific and technical posts. Here the situation is clear: Africans who are being trained at university level are being trained to be teachers (mainly in the humanities) and social workers. They are not being trained to participate at any meaningful level in scientific research.

"Nor can it be said that separate development in education promotes good race relations. The inequalities inherent in the educational system would in themselves be damaging to racial harmony. But one of the aims of the educational system set out in policy statements of both the Government and influential groups in the White sectors of society, is group nationalism. This is translated into the slant of textbooks and has real implications for the co-existence of English and Afrikaner in the same society, as well as implications for the continued harmonious co-existence of Africans, Asians, Coloureds and Whites. In fact, the effects of apartheid on education go far beyond the racial discrimination that the facts and figures of this report demonstrate. The most deplorable effect is on the South African child, whatever his colour and whatever the degree of intellectual capacity developed in him, who, in all cases, is educated within the restrictions of an ideology unacceptable to the world of today."

In the bitter words of one South African, "We studied the White man's language only to learn the terms of our servitude."[19]

This is what apartheid does to education, this is what it seeks to impose on the children of South Africa; those children who must yet grow up to look beyond the barriers of racism and reach out to learn from, and to give to, the whole of mankind.

References in text

1 Dr. W. G. McConkey, former Director of Education in Natal, writing in the *Natal Daily News*, December 1962.

2 *Apartheid, Its Effects on Education, Science, Culture and Information* published by UNESCO, 1967.

3 *Education for Death* by Gregor Ziemer, Constable, London, 1942.

4 Nationalist M. P., Mr. G. F. van L. Froneman, House of Assembly, May 1969.

5 Minister of Indian Affairs, House of Assembly, May 1969.

6 Muriel Horrell, research officer for the South African Institute of Race Relations.

7 *A Survey of Race Relations in South Africa,* 1969 (compiled by M. Horrell, South African Institute of Race Relations).

8 Mr. M. Langschmidt, managing director of Market Research Africa, quoted in *Financial Mail,* 18 April 1969.

9 Mr. P. M. Pillay and Mr. P. A. Ellison, quote in *A Survey of Race Relations in South Africa,* 1969.

10 *African Taxation, Its Relation to African Social Services,* South African Institute of Race Relations, 1960.

11 *The Failure of Bantu Education,* by Dr. W. G. McConkey, a pamphlet published by the Progressive Party in South Africa in 1970, in reply to a Department of Information pamphlet on non-White education.

12 *ibid.*

13 Mr. J. C. M. Mbata, an ex-supervisor of schools, in *Vernacular Tuition,* September 1960.

14 UNESCO.

15 Report, *Rand Daily Mail,* 31 January 1970.

16 Minister of Bantu Education, Mr. W. A. Maree, speaking on 26 June 1959.

17 UNESCO.

18 *Education for Barbarism* by Mr. I. B. Tabata, Prometheus Publications, Durban 1959.

19 *House of Bondage* by Ernest Cole, Allen Lane 1968.

Bibliography

A Survey of Race Relations in South Africa compiled by Muriel Horrell, South African Institute of Race Relations. This is an annual publication and the latest edition is for 1969, published January 1970.

Education For Apartheid by Brian Bunting. A Southern African Education Fund Pamphlet, Christian Action.

Apartheid, Its Effects on Education, Science, Culture and Information, UNESCO in 1967.

A Decade of Bantu Education by Muriel Horrell, South African Institute of Race Relations, 1964.

Education For Isolation, published by the Black Sash, September 1960.

COSMO PIETERSE: Born 1930 in South West Africa. He
graduated from the University of Cape Town, and taught
in Cape Town until leaving South Africa in 1965. He was
banned under the Riotous Assemblies Act, 1962. Mr. Pieterse has compiled and edited *Ten One Act Plays* and is
the co-editor of *Protest and Conflict in African Literature*.
A teacher, poet, dramatist, he now lives in London and is
preparing *Seven South African Poets*.

TRIUMPHAL SONG

"Bayete" they shout, and a thousand more sing
In the echoing thunder: "Our celestial King!"

"Pula! The rain comes. The Raingods arrive"
Is the chorussing burden through the dancing
sounds' drive.

"Was it our prayers," is what they had asked,
"That carried the rain, through the clouds, to our masks,

"After lightning, to fall on parched senses and lands
And stream sweetness on us, hold fruit for our hands?"

"My children, my children," the waters replied,
"The enemy, drought, has been conquered, has died.

"The green of the year that has come, and the clear
Break of day is just what you have made here."

"The spirits reward work, your labour and will
Through those difficult years have ascended and filled

"Heaven with incense, as an offering. The rain
Be at peace is a blessing you earn."

MASSABALALA BONNIE YENGWA ("M.B."): Born 1923, in Natal, South Africa, Secretary of A.N.C. Youth League, 1948; secretary of Natal A.N.C., 1951 and member of the National Executive Committee. In 1953, he was banned from gatherings; 1954, banished from Durban while serving articles as a solicitor. Accused in Treason Trial, 1956; detained after Sharpeville massacre, 1960; detained in solitary confinement 1963, charged with being member of outlawed A.N.C., sentenced to two years imprisonment. While awaiting trial he was admitted as attorney by the Supreme Court. After his release he was placed under house-arrest and again banished. He escaped to Swaziland in 1966 where he practised as solicitor until 1970, when he left for London. Mr. Yengwa is now director of the Lutuli Memorial Foundation.

"THE BANTUSTANS"
South Africa's "Bantu Homelands" Policy

When the White settlers came to South Africa over three hundred years ago, they found the land inhabited by Black and Brown people who were organised into different tribes. Some of these tribes like the Nama and Khoi-khoi were loosely organised living in the Cape Peninsula as nomadic pastoral farmers and hunters. Their lands were taken over by the former settlers without much resistance and their numbers were gradually reduced by disease and killings by the settlers. Soon, however, the settlers had to meet the better organised and more settled

Xhosa who lived on the banks of the Buffalo River. The meeting of the settlers and the Xhosas led to a hundred years' war in which the Xhosas were driven from the Buffalo River to the Fish River. The defeated Xhosas were now to settle in what is known as the Transkei and certain pockets of land between the Kei and Fish River.

The Zulus who inhabited the whole of Natal and parts of the Transvaal, down to the borders of Pondoland fought many battles with the Boer *Voortrekkers* and the English. After their final defeat in 1879 their land was divided up between the English and Boer settlers and only a portion of what is now known as Zululand was left for the occupation of the Zulus. The Zulus living between the Tugela River and Umzimkulu River were also forced into "Native Reserves" scattered between farms owned by Whites. The Orange Free State once occupied by the Basutos is now owned by Whites except for two small areas in Thaba'Nchu and Witzieshoek. In the Transvaal the land once occupied by the Udebeles, Tswanas, Bapedi and Swazis is now almost entirely White owned except for small settlements.

The representatives of the Nationalist Party Government and indeed most White politicians in South Africa maintain that the land that is occupied by the White man in South Africa today was vacant land. According to these White spokesmen Black and White settled in South Africa at the same time and the two groups occupied the lands they presently occupy and therefore the White man is perfectly justified in having the 87 per cent of the land which he found unoccupied when he first came to South Africa.

Nothing could be further from the truth. The fact of the matter is that the African Reserves are shrunken remnants of African land now carved up into many separate blocks whose boundaries were fixed by the conquering White settlers.

The Reserves were supposed to be areas where Africans

could enjoy certain rights and they were areas where Africans could claim the right to ownership of the land. Africans in Reserves however enjoyed no political rights. They had no right to elect members of Parliament and under the South Africa Act of 1909 and the Native Administration Act of 1927 the Governor General (now State President) has power to legislate by proclamation on all matters pertaining to African Reserves. In terms of this legislation he is the Supreme Chief of all Africans in the Reserves and has power to issue orders without prior notice, requiring any tribe or section of a tribe or any African to move from one place to another and not leave any stated area for a specific period.

In most African Reserves the ownership of land is vested in the Native Trust and land is occupied communally by tribesmen who are allotted portions by the Chief in terms of customary procedure and usage. The administration of the Reserves is through the Department of Bantu Affairs and Development. Each district has a Bantu Affairs Commissioner and under the Commissioner are African Chiefs who are in charge of wards. The Chiefs who are paid by the Government, try petty civil and criminal cases and settle disputes relating to allocation of land.

In general the chief occupation of the Reserves is subsistence farming and most areas have not developed beyond the state in which they were over one hundred years ago. Indeed most of them have suffered impoverishment through overcrowding, overstocking and soil erosion.

Not all Africans live in Reserves. There are over 2 million Africans living on White farms – that is, the part of the 87 per cent area of South Africa which is known as belonging to White South Africa. There are African farm labourers in all districts of the Republic, but their number in relation to the White farming population varies from province to province. In Natal there are 16 Africans to 1 White; in the Transvaal the ratio is 6:1. In the Cape the ratio of Coloureds (mixed descent and Africans to Whites is 3.5:1. There are two systems by which an African labourer is employed. One is for a regular monthly wage plus payment in kind, the other is a system of labour tenancy in which there is no cash wage: the African works for a fixed number of days in a year, between 90 and 180 days, in return for the right to live on the farm, to graze cattle, and to cultivate the land.

The African farm labourer enjoys no political rights and because of the insecure position of his employment, he is always looking for opportunities of going out to the African Reserves or to towns.

There are over 3.5 million Africans in urban areas employed in mining, industry, commerce and domestic service. Africans in the mining industry are housed in barracks, called compounds where they stay away from their families until they complete their contracts, which are generally between 9 and 18 months. Africans employed in industry and commerce are either housed in compounds or Bantu Townships. The Townships are made up of rows of sub-standard, identically built houses, usually with two bedrooms. The people rent the houses from the Urban Councils or from the Government. Africans may not acquire freehold rights in these areas and indeed their right to occupy the houses ceases if they become unemployed or "idle" or redundant or if the breadwinner dies and in the case of children, when they reach the age of eighteen years.

Towards the formation of the Union of South Africa in 1910, White South Africans had accepted as a way of life that Black people were inferior beings who therefore could not enjoy the same political and economic rights as the Whites. To maintain their racial attitude of White supremacy or *Wit Baaskap* (White bossmanship) the Blacks had to be segregated from the Whites.

The first legislative enactment embodying the principle of territorial segregation between the Whites and Africans was the Native Land Act of 1913, which in terms of all the former "Native Reserves" in the four provinces were set out in the schedule to the Act and were referred to as "Scheduled Areas". Africans were forbidden from acquiring land outside the Scheduled Areas except by the consent of the Governor General.

This legislation was strongly and vigorously opposed by the African people through their political organisation, the African National Congress. A delegation led by Dr. John L. Dube, the then President General of the A.N.C., went to England to plead with His Majesty's Government to intervene, to protect the rights of the African people. The British Government advised the delegation that they had transferred their rights as guardians of the African interests to the South African Parliament in 1909. This was a sad reminder to the delegation that when self-government was granted to the Whites of South Africa, the political rights of the Black majority were completely ignored.

The Scheduled Areas constituted 10,729,435 morgen (1 morgen is approximately 2 acres). Africans in the Cape Province had enjoyed the right to elect Members of Parliament, and Provincial Council although these members were to be White. In 1936 Dr. J. B. M. Hertzog, then Prime Minister, carried through Parliament legislation which removed Africans from the common voters' roll. Instead they were placed on a separate voters' roll, through which they would elect three White members of the House of Assembly and two White members of the Cape Provincial Council. Africans in the whole country would elect by indirect representation four White Senators to the Senate. This was in a House of Assembly of 153 and a Senate of 46 members. As a *quid pro quo* for removing the Cape Africans from the common voters' roll, Dr. Hertzog councilled the Government to acquire 7,250,000 morgen to be added to the Scheduled Areas. The land would be acquired in terms of the Native Land

and Trust Act of 1936. In terms of this Act, a Native Trust was created, the functions of which were to protect, safeguard and promote the material, moral and social welfare of the Native population and to acquire for Native Settlement the specified area of land. The areas acquired by the Trust were called "Released Areas" and were mostly European or State owned. They were not demarcated so as to consolidate with the Scheduled Areas of the Native Land Act of 1913; as a result there was a development of what became known as "black spots". In 1964 the Minister of Bantu Administration and Development reported that the balance of land still to be acquired in terms of the Native Land and Trust Act of 1936 was 2,031,095 morgen, which means that the land area of African Reserves has increased by only 6,000,000 morgen in the last fifty years.

In terms of the 1936 legislation Africans were to have a Native Representative Council, an elected advisory body, which would advise the Government on matters affecting the Africans. There was widespread opposition to the 1936 legislation. The African National Congress took the initiative in convening an All African Convention, consisting of all organisations in the country. The Convention rejected the terms of the Hertzog 1936 legislation and advised that the institutions created under the Acts should be boycotted. However, leading African personalities decided to give the experiment a trial. They served on it until it was adjourned indefinitely, following the shooting of Africans during the 1946 miners' strike.

When the Nationalist Party Government came to power on the slogan of apartheid and White supremacy or *Wit Baaskap*, they immediately set about introducing rigid apartheid within the so-called White Areas. They introduced separate entrances to railway stations, separate queues in public counters and separate buses and trains, etc. They then appointed the Tomlinson Commission which gave its report in 1954. It soon became clear that the apartheid policy of the Government is based on certain fundamental assumptions which can be summarised as follows:

1 In the White Areas – that is, 87 per cent of the land area of South Africa, Africans will never enjoy equal rights with the Whites.
2 Africans will be given self-government in their own areas. Africans, however are not one nation but various nations and therefore each Bantu National Group must be given its "separate freedom".
3 Africans must therefore go back to their Homelands and Whites must learn to do without African labour.
4 Development plans must be speeded up to make the Homelands economically viable. It is the duty of the White government to assist African Homelands to attain this objective.

In pursuance of the above objectives the South African Government passed the Bantu Authorities Act of 1951 which was designed to replace the old system of Local Councils in terms of which the Transkeian "Bunga", officially known as the Transkeian Territories General Council, was formed. It offered more authority to Africans themselves. It made provision for the establishments of Bantu tribal, regional and territorial authorities and for the gradual delegation to these authorities of certain executive and administrative powers including the levying of rates. In terms of this Act the Natives Representative Council established under the Hertzog 1936 legislation was abolished.

During the years that followed, opposition to the Bantu Authorities Act grew and in some cases erupted into violent clashes where many lives were lost.

Leading the struggle against the Bantu Authorities system was the African National Congress, which had over the years fought valiantly against segregation and its result of injustice and human suffering. The great Defiance Campaign against the Unjust Laws of 1952 had been directed, among other things, against the policy of apartheid and Bantustans.

The South African Government literature on Bantustans and Bantu Homelands gives the reader the impression that this policy is not only acceptable to the African people, but also a product of joint consultation between the parties and is the result of their mutual decisions. Nothing could be further from the truth.

In the Transkei (the first Bantustan and Government's model), opposition to the Bantu Authorities erupted into an armed revolt by the peasants of Pondoland in 1960. The revolt was also directed against the Government and the Chiefs who had agreed to complement the Government's policy. The Government tried hard to convey the impression that all was well in Pondoland except for trouble caused by a few agitators. It soon became clear, however, that the revolt had assumed a mass character and the Government issued the now notorious Emergency Proclamation 400 of 1960, which gave police powers to detain anyone indefinitely without trial. The most telling answer against the Government's claim that Bantustans enjoy the full support of the people of the Transkei is that the Emergency Proclamation 400 is still in force and that to this date people are held in custody in terms of the Proclamation.

According to Government sources 4,769 men and women were held in custody for indefinite periods of time during 1960. Of this number, 2,067 were eventually brought to trial (House of Assembly Debate, 27 January 1961).

The popular movement headed by a committee known as the Mountain Committee which started in the district of Bizana, spread to other districts in Pondoland. Many *kraals* or homes of Government informers were burnt down and many Chiefs and sub-Chiefs who supported the Government were killed. The most serious clash between the opponents of Bantu Authorities and the Government forces occurred at Ngquza Hill, between Bizana and Lusikisiki.

As peasants were meeting to consider their common problems resulting from the introduction of Bantu Authorities, two aircraft and a helicopter suddenly appeared and dropped tear-gas and smoke bombs on the crowd. Simultaneously, police emerged from all directions and surrounded the meeting. The meeting raised a white flag to show that it was a peaceful one, but the police suddenly opened fire, killing eleven people. Subsequently, at an inquest on the shootings, the magistrate declared that the firing of sten-gun bullets was "unjustified and excessive, even reckless". Several of the men shot by the police had bullet wounds through the backs of their heads.

In the Orange Free State, there are only two small Bantu Homelands whose total area is not more than 77,000 morgen. In one of these Homelands, Witzieshoek, there were clashes between the people and the police in 1950 as a result of the peasants' opposition to Bantu Authorities. During the disturbances fourteen Africans were shot dead and two policemen were killed. (*The Cape Times*, 27 November 1950.) The leaders of the people including Chief Paulus Mopeli, were deported. Some leaders have now been allowed to return to Witzieshoek after agreeing to carry out Government policy.

In the Transvaal, the people of Sekhukhuniland rose up against the Government's Bantu Authorities Act in 1957. Several men of the tribe, including the Chief and his nearest relatives, were exiled to distant areas in Natal and the Transkei. Some of the men were still living in exile in 1969.

Because the Government had deposed the Chief for his opposition of Bantu Authorities, riots broke out in several villages and some Government supporters were killed. More than two hundred people were arrested in one incident alone and at the trial eleven people were sentenced to death, including the Chieftainess. The sentences were later converted to life sentences.

In Zululand, the Government had by substantial propaganda tried to win the support of the Paramount Chief, King Cyprian Bhekuzulu Ka Solomon, and his sub-Chiefs. The then Minister of Native Affairs called a great *Undata* (meeting) at the Nougama in 1957 where he personally presented the idea of the Bantustans. The Zulus politely thanked him for his generosity and then requested him to bring back King Cetshwayos' crown, which was taken away when the Zulus were defeated in 1879. This was a way of indicating to the Minister that they did not believe in his "self-government".

Soon after this meeting however, the Paramount Chief, in his capacity as Chief of the Usutu tribe of the Zulus accepted Bantu Authorities. This was strongly opposed by his tribesmen.

In the district of Tokazi, there was so much opposition that clashes took place between those who accepted Bantu Authorities and those who opposed it. As a result of these clashes two of the supporters of Bantu Authorities were killed and twenty-nine tribesmen were charged with murder. Of this number fourteen were convicted of murder and sentenced to various terms of imprisonment. In his remarks, the presiding trial judge observed that it was clear that there was deep resentment against Bantu Authorities and that the Government had been aware of this but had imposed the scheme in spite of the opposition.

Despite the overwhelming opposition of the people and their political organisations the Government has gone on with ruthlessness and force, introducing Bantu Authorities throughout South Africa.

There is hardly an area where Bantu Authorities has not been established. In all instances it is the Chiefs, the paid agents of the Government, who are the cornerstone of Bantu Authorities. Their position in Bantu Authorities' organisation is entrenched in that they are appointed by the

Government and in Bantu Authorities constitutions they form the majority of the membership. As mentioned above, Bantu Authorities has been forced and imposed upon the African people in virtually every Bantu Homeland where it has been established. Those leaders who profess to support it either do so because they genuinely believe that by supporting it they will plant the seeds of its own destruction or because they have opted for short term personal and tribal gains. The Government pays handsomely those tribes and "leaders" who support apartheid and Bantustans.

Let us now try to examine the rationale of the Bantustan policy, and find out whether it stands the test of equity and justice on which it is supposed to be based.

Leaders of the various Nationalist governments have repeatedly asserted that in the White Areas, that is 87 per cent of South Africa, Africans will never enjoy equal rights with Whites. In Parliament on 24 April 1968 Mr. B. J. Vorster, Prime Minister of South Africa, said, "They (the Africans) remain there (in White Areas) because they cannot provide employment for themselves. But the fact that you employ those people does not place you under an obligation to grant them political rights ... Surely the fact remains that working for a man does not give you the right to run his affairs ... It is true that there are Blacks working for us. They will continue to work for us for generations, in spite of the ideal, we have to separate them completely ... The fact of the matter is this: we need them because they work for us but after all, we pay them for their work ... But the fact that they work for us can never ... entitle them to claim political rights. Not now, nor in the future ... under no circumstances can we grant them those political rights in our own territory, neither now nor ever."

Earlier, Dr. H. F. Verwoerd, elaborating on the policy of apartheid said, "To say that economic integration exists simply because Africans were employed in factories and on farms ... then the asses, oxen and tractors were also integrated, because they too were indispensable."

In an attempt to justify their policy of denying Africans basic human rights, Nationalist leaders assert that 87 per cent of South Africa belongs to White South Africa because when they arrived here they found it unoccupied and they then developed it themselves. Of course they were assisted in their efforts by Natives, asses, oxen and tractors. Natives cannot complain however because the Whites "paid" them for their work, and they were also doing them a favour because "they cannot provide employment for themselves."

Of course this Nationalist way of thinking only succeeds to expose their racial prejudice and their regard of Africans as inferior beings, and Whites as superior beings. Africans have always lived in the so-called White Areas since the Whites came to South Africa. At the very moment there are more Africans than Whites in these so-called White Areas than there are in the so-called Black Areas or Bantu Homelands.

White immigrants into the White Areas qualify to all the rights of citizenship between three and five years. A newly arrived White immigrant is not subject to job-reservation. He is not subject to restrictions of movement from one area to another and from influx control. He is free to join trade unions and to own property and to engage in the occupation of his choice, simply because of the accident of his birth with a white skin. The country of his birth is in the main irrelevant. It is his white skin that matters and not whether he was born in Hungary, Germany, France, England or the United States.

The idea that South African development has been dependent on White effort alone with Africans playing the same role as asses, oxen and tractors is not only unjust and ungrateful but inhuman and deceitful. Africans, living in the Bantu Homelands and in the so-called White Areas have spent the best part of their lives building and developing South African industry through their labour and effort. Africans have been loyally giving their skill and labour to South African industry and commerce despite the fact that all opportunities to promotion to skilled and managerial jobs were closed to them. They were loyal in spite of the fact that their wages compared with Whites doing the same job were less than 33.3 per cent and the difference between those skilled workers (White) and unskilled workers (Black) was more than 70 per cent. This is the discrimination on the grounds of colour which the Nationalist Government seeks to clothe under the policy of Bantu Homelands and Bantustans.

The tragedy of South Africa is that White racial arrogance and exclusiveness has driven the present Government to the policy of Bantustans, and is accepted by the vast majority of White South Africans. The stubborn refusal of their leaders to consider any negotiations for the granting of political and economic rights to Africans makes the solution of the racial situation in South Africa one of the most complex in history. One may ask, how are leaders of African liberation to deal with a government whose leader has declared, "Under no circumstances can we grant them (Africans) those political rights in our own territory, neither now nor ever." It appears clear to the writer at least that in order to make the South African Government realise that human rights cannot be divided on the grounds of colour, force will have to be used.

The pillar of apartheid and Bantustans is the assumption that Africans have their Homelands. Before the Nationalists coined the sweet sounding terms of "Bantu Homelands" and Bantustans, these areas were known as Native or Bantu Reserves. No doubt the word Bantu Reserve was the more descriptive term. Rightly it immediately brings to mind areas set aside for other things in South Africa – "Game and Native Reserves".

Like game reserves, the Homelands have always been regarded as places where the Africans could be seen in their "natural, unspoilt surroundings". Like game reserves, "strangers" may not be admitted without a permit and residents may not leave the reserve without a permit. Animals in game reserves cannot make decisions for themselves as they do not have the power of rational thinking. In the African Reserves decisions about development are taken by the White Government and their officials. All animals belong to a game reserve and the fact that they are sometimes brought out of the reserve for entertainment and other uses, will never change their status. When the animals are no longer of use to humans outside the game reserve they have to be sent back to it – by force.

According to South African Government policy all Africans belong to the Reserves. It does not matter where they were born and where they have spent their lives. If they have been outside the Reserves it has been for the benefit of the Whites only and they may only remain there as long as their labour is required by the Whites. If they fall sick or grow old or for any other reason become redundant then they must go back to the Reserves where they belong. Africans should not be a burden of the White man, where he does not belong – he should go back to his own people who should look after him. He is only a temporary sojourner.

Before the accession of the Nationalist Party to power, the African Reserves were recognised for what they are: reservoirs for cheap, unskilled labour. They had never been developed, because it was impossible to develop them when over 70 per cent of its active male population spent its life working in White industries. Over the years they had become overcrowded and impoverished rural slums.

The Nationalist Government however, saw in the Reserves their answer to their plan to segregate the races on the basis of their colour. The Whites who have the vote would remain in the areas they occupy, but all Africans outside the Reserves, numbering over 6 million, would have to go back to the Reserves now given the new and pleasant sounding name of "Homelands". To prepare the ground for this momentous task the Government set up a Commission of Inquiry in 1950 under the Chairmanship of Professor Tomlinson. This Commission reported in 1954 and is popularly known by the name of its Chairman as the Tomlinson Commission.

Let us now take a closer look at the areas which are planned to accommodate all the 14 million Africans of the Republic.*

The Transkei

According to the Tomlinson Commission the total area of the Transkei is 4,944,517 morgen. This is the largest compact area for African occupation. Its people, though divided into different tribes, are all Xhosa speaking. Of this area, 963,870 morgen are considered White agricultural areas. This is the area mainly in Mount Currie, Matatiele, Elliot, Maclean and Port St. Johns districts and in towns and parts of towns that are still zoned for White ownership and occupation.

Topographically the Transkei is very broken country. Three-quarters of the land is very mountainous or very hilly and only 11 per cent can be classed as gently rolling or flat. The roughness of the terrain is firstly caused by the mountain ranges, but also the five principal rivers, which with their tributaries, run through the territory eating out deep valleys.

The Deputy Minister of Bantu Administration said in the Assembly on 3 June 1969, that the *de facto* African population of the Transkei (excluding absent workers) is

* For the following descriptions I have relied heavily on the booklet entitled *The African Reserves of South Africa*, published by the South African Institute of Race Relations.

about 1,579,000 at any one time. The *de jure* population also included 233,000 migratory workers and 1,029,000 living outside the Transkei, giving a combined total of 2,841,000. The Tomlinson Commission reported in 1954 that the density of the population was 82 per square mile (excluding absentees) with a fairly even spread. When the Commission reported only 26 per cent of the land was free from soil erosion.

Umtata, the principal town, is connected to the railway system of the Cape, while Mataliele and Kokstad are linked to the Natal system. The only African territory that this line crosses is Umzimkulu. A line linking Sterkstroom and Maclean runs fairly near the Transkeian border. A National road runs through the territory, connecting with a network of reasonably good gravel roads. The only harbour, Port St. Johns, has been zoned for Whites. It is badly silted up.

In nineteen of the twenty-six districts the land is occupied under communal tenure, individual tenure being in force in the rest in so far as arable plots are concerned. In the latter areas plot holders pay an annual quitrent. The principle of "one man – one plot" applies. Subdivision is controlled, the land may not be disposed of without official permission and it may be forfeited if the owner is convicted of certain crimes or fails to pay his quitrent or on account of non-beneficial occupation. The land may not be mortgaged or pledged nor may it be sold in execution of a debt.

"Mixed farming is practised, with a bias to cattle." The Commission found that in the Transkei and other high rainfall zones of mixed farming areas 96 per cent of the cultivated land was under maize and Kaffircorn or millet, the yield averaging 3.9 bags per morgen and 8.6 bags per family. Thirteen per cent of the farmers possessed more than 20 units of stock, 63 per cent 10 or less; 32 per cent 4 or less and 15 per cent possessed no stock at all. Twelve per cent of the farmers made more than £120 per year out of their farming and 44 per cent made less than £40.

The Ciskei

The Ciskei consists of seventeen pieces of land with a total area of 1,035,903 morgen. The Tomlinson Commission stated that these areas formed no coherent whole, but were merely an administrative unit. The largest blocks of land are in Herschel, Glen Grey, King William's Town, Keiskawmahoek, Whittlesea and Peddie districts.

When the Commission reported, there were twenty-four pieces of land: various "black spots" have been removed, for example one in the Hamansdorp district, the Newlands location about fifteen miles north of East London, two other areas in the same district and tribal farms in Cathcart, Kourgha and other areas. The Government has bought numbers of farms from Whites in the King William's Town, Keiskawmahoek, and Peddie areas, with the ultimate of moving Africans to the west of the main road and railway line linking East London with the interior, leaving a White corridor along this line and along the coast for some distance on each side of East London.

The railway line linking East London to Port Elizabeth passes through African territory in the Middledrift area.

The country is drier than the Transkei and almost like desert in certain areas.

The Commission reported that the population density was 78 per square mile. In areas like Herschel, Keiskawmahoek and Glen Grey density was as high as 100 per square mile. Herschel was found to be one of the most badly eroded areas of the whole country.

Individual tenure is in force in the Glen Grey district and several surveyed locations elsewhere. Otherwise the allocation of land is on a communal basis under the control of the Bantu Affairs Commissioner, who acts in consultation with the Chief or headman.

The Deputy Minister of Bantu Development said in the Assembly on 21 April 1968 that there were more than two hundred unconsolidated Bantu Areas in Natal. He added that the Government did not regard complete consolidation of these areas as being possible in the foreseeable future. The total area of these tracts of land is about 3,718,000 morgen.

Large-scale removal schemes have been in progress in the effort to achieve some degree of consolidation and large numbers of so-called black spots have been eliminated in farms like Meran, Lyell, Hlatikulu and farms in the Waschbank, Klip River, Bulwer, Underberg, Umkomaas Valley, Newcastle and Dannhauser areas. These removals which are carried out without consultation of the African people and in which they have no choice but to comply with the Government order to move, have caused untold hardship among the African people. The Africans removed from the areas mentioned are being resettled on land adjoining Reserves in the Dundee district or in villages or closer settlements near Newcastle and elsewhere.

According to the Tomlinson Commission 58 per cent of the land in Bantu Areas of Natal is mountainous. The areas in Northern Zululand and Tongoland are semi-highlands or coastal flats; in the latter regions the climate is very hot and unhealthy and the country is very thinly populated. The highlands (except for their deep bushy valleys) have a much more pleasant climate and could be very productive, especially if irrigated.

The higher land of the Tugela region is bushy country, suitable for cattle, with moderate possibilities for irrigation. Because of the mountainous nature of the land, dryland cultivation can be practised in selected areas only.

A third group of Bantu Areas lies in a wide arc along

the foothills of the Drakensberg mountains. Numbers of these have been eliminated under black spot removal schemes. These Reserves are much overpopulated.

The fourth group of Bantu Areas lies on the southern semi-coastal region, with hilly terrain. They have a mild climate with good rainfall and are naturally suited to various types of farming. However the population density is extremely high: up to 350 to 400 per square mile in the Umlazi Reserve in 1954. The average population density for the Bantu Areas in Natal in 1954 was 82 per square mile.

Except on Mission Reserves, the allocation of land is made by Chiefs and headmen, subject to the authority and supervision of the White Bantu Affairs Commissioner, and in accordance with Government regulations. In the Mission Reserves land is communally held, except in a few individual cases where it is held under freehold tenure on Mission farms like Amanzumtoti, Uluooti and Imfawe. It is held under leasehold tenure in other Mission farms like those near Amanzumtoti, at Imjume, Impapa and Ifafa. The Reserves are mainly cattle country. All the main roads and railway lines pass through "White corridors".

The Western Transvaal and Northern Cape Tswana Areas

These consist of six large and a number of smaller blocks. The area is altogether 4,330,135 morgen in extent.

In these areas there have been large-scale removal schemes from tribal farms and smaller Reserves. Africans have had to leave such near Rustenburg, Ventersdorp, Potchefstroom, Koster and other places, being removed to land adjoining large Reserves in the Swartruggens, Lichtenburg, and Northern Rustenburg districts. In the Northern Cape, people from near Kimberly, Barkly West and Mafeking and surrounding areas have been resettled on land next to large blocks of African Reserves in the Taung or Kuruman districts or adjoining the Malopo Reserve to the west of Mafeking.

According to the Bulletin of the African Institute for April 1969 the official plan is that the Tswana in the Northern Cape and Western Transvaal should eventually be concentrated in six main areas: in the Vryburg-Kuruman, Mafeking, Marico, Rustenburg, Brits-Warmbaths and Bronkhorstspruit districts.

There is another group of about 50,000 Tswana at Thaba'Nchu in the Orange Free State. In 1951 the total for the other areas was 314,402. The population density averages about 26 per square mile. The land is held under communal tenure. The country becomes progressively drier towards the west and south where stock farming only is possible. To the east livestock farming is coupled with irregular cultivation, mainly of Kaffircorn and millet.

The Tomlinson Commission reported that in the pastoral farming regions the average yield of grain is only 0.6 bags per morgen or 2.5 bags per family a year. Twenty-four per cent of the farmers own more than 20 units of stock, 38 per cent more than 10 units; 38 per cent 10 units or less and 8 per cent less than 5 units. Only 1 per cent own no livestock at all. Nineteen per cent of the farmers made more than £60 a year out of their farming and 37 per cent made less than £20. The principal roads and railway lines in the Tswana regions pass mainly through "White" territory, but do traverse African Reserves to the north of Rustenburg, to the south of Mafeking and near Taung.

The Northern Areas Bapedi, Venda, Shangane and other Tribes

The Reserves in the Northern and Eastern Transvaal have a combined area of 4,292,850 morgen. They consist of eight large and a number of smaller blocks. Except for small stretches, the railway lines and main roads traverse the White Areas between the Reserves.

As in other regions, black spot removal schemes have been in progress in these areas. Africans have been moved for example from farms in the Middleburg and Groblersdal district to land adjoining the Sekhukhuneland Reserve; from Wallmansthal north-east of Pretoria to land to the west in the Harmanskraal area; and from Eersterus, near Pretoria, to Trust farms in the Harmanskraal area. There has been another type of removal scheme within the Reserves themselves: of tribal groups who are living amongst Africans of different racial origin.

There are probably about 1.5 million Africans in these Reserves, but the exact number is not known. There are a considerable number of ethnic groups in these areas consisting of Tswana, Bapedi, Ndebele, Tsonga, Venda and Swazi.

Roughly half of the total area of the Northern Reserves is flat or softly undulating middle-veld or dry bush-veld country, less than 500 feet in height, with a average rainfall of between 15 and 20 inches a year. Periods of severe drought occur. The rest of the area is mountainous or hilly.

Large, scattered tracts of land are tribally owned, but the greater proportion is owned by the South Africa Nature Trust, where control of occupation is exercised by officials of the Department of Bantu Administration and Development according to a form of leasehold tenure. These Reserves are cattle country in the main, although mixed farming is possible in areas of higher rainfall. The average dryland maize yield is stated to vary from 3 to 6 bags per morgen.

The Southern Sotho Area of Witzieshoek

This is a small Bantu Reserve in the east of the Province of the Orange Free State. It is mountainous country inhabited by Africans of Sotho origin. The land is occupied under communal tenure. It is cattle country although mixed farming is possible in some parts.

It will be noticed that whilst the Reserves vary in size and population content, they have many similar features. The most obvious is of course that they are called Bantu Reserves. This means that by law and practice these areas are reserved for "Bantu" people only. Incidentally the word "Bantu" is a name given to the African people by the Nationalist Government and now accepted by most South African Whites as correct address for the aboriginal people of South Africa. They use it in preference to the old name "Native" or "Kaffir" to which they have been told the Bantu take exception. Africans, of course, call themselves Africans, which they are. This word, however, has now been adopted by the White section of the population who call themselves "Afrikaners" and according to South African Whites it would be as much an insult to call "Bantu" Africans as to call White people Black. The South African White's feelings of superiority towards Africans are pathological. The very word "Bantu" in a sense connotes in the minds of most Whites an inferior status. Thus to their White vanity the South African Government has legislated for separate "Bantu" Education with separate "Bantu" universities to produce "Bantu" lawyers, "Bantu" doctors and "Bantu" graduates. The enthusiasm for the creation of separate "Bantu" Homelands out of the "Bantu" Reserves must be seen as an extension of the same type of mental attitude.

The South African Government tries hard to deny that its policies are motivated by feelings of racial prejudice and White domination. Yet all major economic developments in South Africa have taken place in so-called White Areas and the Reserves have been sadly neglected only serving as reservoirs of cheap labour for White Areas.

The next and perhaps most important feature of the

Reserves is their abject poverty which has ground people into a position of indifference and apathy. Most have even despaired of trying to improve their position which seems impossible to change by their effort and endeavour. The mass of statistics and objective description of the physical features, density of population and climatic conditions cannot tell the full story of the conditions in the African Reserves. Here grinding poverty and the resulting malnutrition, disease and squalor have become a way of life. This is the land of women, children and old and sick people. The healthy and active are the only exports the Reserves have in the form of cheap "Bantu" labour which they sell to the mining, agricultural and secondary industries in the White Areas. In the Reserves – all Reserves – famine and starvation are the usual seasonal visitations. These are the areas where the well-off earn £60 per year and many others earn less than £10 per year.

The "poor Whites" earn more than ten times the earnings of the "well-off" Africans in Reserves. The bulk of the population in the Reserves is poor because most of the land itself is unsuitable for farming. The little that is suitable is too small for the population to make a living out of it. Because the land is overcrowded it has become eroded and progressively impoverished with the result that its yield has diminished instead of increasing. The system of communal occupation of land under the tribal system inhibits initiative and the adoption of modern methods of soil tillage. The system itself is insecure and does not encourage a farmer to invest capital and apply effort in an area where he may be moved at the whim and fancy of government officials. Because people from the Reserves have never been accepted as permanent residents, they have been migratory labourers, strangers both in the Reserves and White towns.

These are the "Homelands" where the Government of South Africa has ordered that another 6 million Africans from White Areas must be moved. Obviously the immediate question is, how could this be accomplished in the face of these appalling conditions of poverty and decay?

The South African Government says that it has found the answer in the development of Reserves and border industries.

In terms of development plans, no need for additional land existed, all that was necessary was to make the Reserves support the increased population.

The Tomlinson Commission which was charged by the Nationalist Government with the task of investigating the possibilities of making segregation work within the present apartheid borders was faced with this problem of reconciling the increased population of the Reserves with their level of production. It realised that agricultural rehabilitation in the Reserves could not take place in isolation. It stressed that essential pre-conditions for agricultural reform were general economic development providing employment to relieve the pressure of population upon the land and social development to produce a climate of opinion in which reform could be possible. The Commission submitted proposals which it estimated could increase the carrying capacity of the Reserves to 10 million people within twenty-five to thirty years. But even if this were accomplished it calculated that there would then be some 6 million Africans in White Areas.

According to the Commission an African family in the Reserves requires on the average 52.5 morgen of land to make a gross annual income of £70. It proceeded to recommend that arable and residential plots should be sold to individual Africans and that the purchasers should be granted conditional freehold titles. The speedy revision of the system of land tenure was a prerequisite for the Commission's whole scheme of economic development. The Government however, rejected these recommendations on the ground that they would undermine the whole tribal structure. At that time it also rejected another major proposal, to the effect that White entrepreneurs should, subject to certain conditions, be invited to establish industries within the Reserves as well as on their borders. The Government has now come round to accept the principle of establishing border industries established with White capital and entrepreneurship.

There has been development in the Reserves since the publication of the Tomlinson Commission Report, but it is not of the type that would make the Reserves viable and able to support their existing population, let alone the population that is being forced to go there under the Homelands Scheme. The Reserves in general still cannot produce enough food for their inhabitants. It has been shown that in the year 1953-54 of the average food consumption per family costing approximately £60 per year, only half came from sources within the Reserves; the balance of the food had to be acquired beyond the borders of the Reserves through the sale of Reserve labour.

The idea of making Reserves viable and economically independent of White South Africa is impossible of achievement in as much as it is not possible to run the South African economy without Africans.

Racial interdependence of the South African economy is a fact which in itself no one could quarrel about. What makes Africans object to apartheid most strongly is that it is always the Blacks who must sacrifice in order to make apartheid work. The sacrifice is being made not in exchange for some expected future gain but to satisfy White vainglory and colour prejudice. However although development of the Homelands is supposed to be for the benefit of the African people themselves, hardly any attention is paid to their own views and desires.

Writing on this J. E. Spence* has said: "In South Africa not even lip-service is paid to the idea of consultation and

* J. E. Spence, *African Affairs Journal*, Vol. 59, April 1960, page 139.

discussion between interested parties. Recently we witnessed the spectacle of the South African Government voicing open disapproval at the desire of certain prominent SABRA (South African Bureau of Racial Affairs) officials to discuss Government policy with leaders of African political organisations. This refusal is bitterly resented ... The argument that only the Government in each case is in a responsible position to decide the nature and scope of political, economic and social arrangements for non-White peoples must be rejected on the grounds that the latter feel themselves at the mercy of a small ruling elite who will only legislate in their own interests. What other conclusions can non-White opinion draw when little or no attention is paid to their wishes, whether expressed or not. What rights non-Whites do possess are seen to be at the mercy of an alien legislative process and the record of the last ten years has seen a progressive deterioration in these rights in the name of 'Apartheid'.

"Furthermore, the assumption of sole legislative responsibility by the White ruling group in the name of a political and social doctrine has destroyed in the minds of the rulers any feeling that they are in fact dealing with individual lives of thousands of human beings."

It is this point of lack of respect of the human personality and human dignity which makes the Government policy of apartheid so detestable and abominable to the African people. No African political organisation worthy of its name has ever supported segregation and apartheid. Africans did not create the "Homelands", they did not create "black spots" nor did they invent the word apartheid. Yet when the policy of apartheid has to be carried out it would appear at least to date that it is Africans who have to bear the burden of making the policy work. It is the Africans who must be moved from black spots to consolidated Reserves. The black spot removal schemes now being carried out in many parts of the country are a manifestation of one of the greatest human tragedies of our time. They constitute a ruthless operation against a voiceless and defenceless people, to deprive them of their rights to occupation or ownership of the lands, some of which they had occupied from time immemorial. It is an operation which is cynical and heartless, which is herding thousands of Africans, through bribery, deception and even brutal force, to overcrowded Reserves where they cannot conceivably be able to support themselves through agriculture and where there are no opportunities of employment.

The Government has admitted that it would be impossible to form all African areas into solid blocks for each "nation" and yet the Government has decreed that all smaller isolated African black spots must be ruthlessly eliminated. This is done to satisfy a cynical, partisan and inhuman political ideology of race separation or apartheid or *Wit Baaskap* or whatever other term that fits into the South African political vocabulary for its policy of oppressing the Black people in South Africa. Removal schemes are carried out not for the benefit of the Africans but for the benefit of the White apartheid god, which feeds on a rare diet called "apartheid", and for the last twenty years it has been demanding from its worshippers more and more of this diet and as it waxes fat and obese, it threatens death and destruction to the White adherents if apartheid is not delivered to it in bigger and bigger chunks. To the White Government and its supporters it is of no consequence that some of these lands were individual, tribal and Mission farms where Africans had lived peacefully for over four generations and that the people bought the land in good faith over a hundred years ago. Neither does it matter to them that some of these areas were officially set aside by the Government for African occupation and proclaimed as African Reserves under the 1913 Land Act and under the Native Land and Trust Act of 1936.

In the black spot removal and Homelands schemes, the

Government is involved in a human drama full of tragedy and cruelty that causes one to shudder at the thought of the long term effect it will have in the relations between Black and White peoples of the world. The Government in its propaganda hand-outs states that Africans in the black spots are moving voluntarily. We have listed in these pages cases of resistance to Bantu Authorities, removals and "betterment schemes" where leaders have been imprisoned and Government supporters were in some cases killed. This does not appear to be a voluntary operation. Cosmas Desmond* in his book on removals lists a number of instances where "volunteers" for removal schemes, such as the case of the Bakubung people who refused to move from Leding and that of the residents of Morajo and Thaba'Nchu who were opposed to moving, went to the Supreme Court. However, they were ordered by the Courts to comply with the order.

Mr. Desmond correctly argues in his book that even if people volunteered to move, there would be no excuse for moving people to places where there are no houses, no basic facilities and no local employment. In his investigations he found that the lack of employment applied even to many of the better townships in the Reserves where houses and some other facilities are provided.

Dr. P. Smit, at the Congress on Geography Education (*Star*, 11 July 1969) said that many of the sixty-five "towns" being developed in the Homelands had no economic basis and that if no industries were established near these "towns" they would develop into little more than settlements of women and children with the men earning a living in the White towns. At present he said more than 40 per cent of the economically active men are absent from Homelands at any given time.

The enforced resettlement schemes are forcing a split-

* *The Discarded People* by C. Desmond, published by the Christian Institute of South Africa, pages 18-19.

ting up of African families because the White economy demands the presence of the African workers in urban areas, and the apartheid ideology demands that as many Africans as possible must live in their Homelands.

Mr. G. F. Van L. Froneman M. P., Deputy Chairman of the Bantu Affairs Commission, said in the House of Assembly on 6 February 1968, "We are trying to introduce the migratory labour pattern as far as possible in every sphere, that is in fact the entire basis of our policy as far as the White economy is concerned." Thus it can be seen that for the sake of the White man's comfort, the Black man must be deprived of his right to live with his wife and family.

In the face of all evidence that African Reserves or Homelands are not economically viable and cannot support their present population even on subsistence standards; and further, when malnutrition, poverty and starvation are part of the way of life in the Reserves, one is driven to question seriously the *bona fides* of the White Government and to wonder whether there is not a plan to maintain White nationhood at the expense of the African Nation, even to the extent of decreasing the numbers of the African people through economic strangulation by herding them to starving Reserves. Obviously the South African Government will vehemently deny the charge that they plan to weaken and/or exterminate the African people through economic strangulation. However this belief is further substantiated by another ideological-political campaign carried out by the Nationalist Government with vigour and thoroughness.

Those who know something about South African history will remember that long before it was fashionable to speak about White unity and the White Nation, the African people from different tribes, the Xhosas, Zulus, Sothos, Swazis, Shanganes, Tswanas and others met in Bloemfontein in 1912 and decided to form themselves into one nation – an African Nation and then and there formed the

African National Congress, their political mouthpiece. Since 1912 the African National Congress has waged its struggle for the liberation of the African people as a united people. Its leadership to this day is composed of men and women from all the tribes of South Africa who serve the people not according to tribal origin or affiliation but as Africans. The White Government in 1966 suddenly discovered it was not safe to regard all Africans as one Bantu group. It made them appear strong and superior. In 1966 the Minister of Bantu Administration and Development defined his object as the chief priest of apartheid, "To give to every Bantu Nation in accordance with its national character . . . I want . . . to bring a most interesting point to the attention of all of us . . . As regards all the various nations we have here, the *White Nation*, the *Coloured Nation*, the *Indian Nation*, the various *Bantu Nations*, something to which we have given too little regard is the fact that *numerically the White Nation is superior* to all other nations in South Africa." He then proceeded to try and show that this "has a very wide implication for us all . . . Firstly it demonstrates the utter folly of saying that a minority government is ruling others in South Africa . . . It demonstrates our duty as guardians . . . Our policy is based on facts . . . of separateness and diversity of the various *Bantu Nations* and other nations in South Africa as separate national groups set on separate courses to separate destinies." He concluded that "in the final instance our work is directed at eventual geographic partition".

The suggestion by White South Africa that the Africans in South Africa consist of many nations has particular significance in the development of their apartheid, *Baaskap* ideology. It helps them to see themselves as a "White Nation" with a majority of numbers and therefore perfectly entitled to dominate other nations with smaller populations. It would then be "utter folly" to say "that a minority government is ruling others in South Africa". It would also satisfy the national propensity of the Whites of the feeling of superiority over the Black people. It would therefore be right that the Whites should govern the Blacks because they are superior in everything including numbers.

One wonders whether it ever occurred to the Minister when he made the statement that he was Minister of "Bantu" Administration and not Zulu, Xhosa and Sotho administration.

Since South Africa became an independent state in 1910, Africans, irrespective of their tribal origin have been subject to the same laws and have been subject to the same administration. The Minister had not consulted Africans to find out how many nations they had wanted to become. This was one of the many cases where Africans are told what is good for them without any prior consultation. The suspicion is that the Minister of Bantu Administration based his astounding theory on the grounds that Africans belong to many tribes which speak different dialects. This argument cannot be sustained, however, because Whites also belong to different "tribes" or nationalities from Europe and Asia. (In the case of Asia I include Japanese, who are classed as honorary Whites in South Africa.) The "Indian Nation" also consists of various tribes and national groups, the most important being Hindus and Pakistanis. The "Coloured Nation" would have people from different backgrounds, Indian, African and White. The right to qualify as a nation according to Mr. Botha must be something else besides common language, history, culture and customs.

It seems the overriding factor is the necessity for dividing Africans into smaller and manageable units and thus apply more efficiently the old technique of divide and rule.

It is interesting that this type of thinking should come from a Government that has been protesting that the world fails to appreciate their problem and their method of solving the race problem because the world does not realise that they are outnumbered by Africans in the ratio of 3:1. Even though their numbers are now superior to all South African nations they must still practise apartheid and race discrimination. Perhaps they will soon discover another plausible reason why the world should not judge them harshly on their practice of segregation.

The development of the Bantustan idea has been slow judging by the tremendous efforts on the part of the Government to make it acceptable to the African people. It is now nearly twenty years since the Bantu Authorities Act was passed in 1951, and yet there is not a single Bantu Homeland that enjoys genuine independence.

There are two main reasons for this. Firstly, Africans have been aware all the time that independence promised by the Government even if genuine, would be unfair because they will have to be segregated into 13 per cent of the land and this is the least developed part of the country. They were aware that this offer for independence was not made out of generosity and good heart on the part of the Whites, but was an attempt to extricate them from the responsibility of granting the Africans fundamental human rights in South Africa.

Secondly, the Government is faced with the problem of granting independence to an African Government. The South African Government still wants segregation or apartheid practised even in the Homelands and also to dominate the Bantustan Governments.

To illustrate our point, apartheid is practised in the Transkei and it is practised, as in the rest of South Africa to the advantage of the White man. After seven years of "self-government" the Transkei has not been given the portfolios of Internal Security, Foreign Affairs and Defence. Clearly self-government without these key departments is still a hollow sham.

When Dr. H. F. Verwoerd, the Prime Minister, was speaking over the Promotion of the Bantu Self-Government Bill which became law in 1959, he made it clear that although large numbers of Africans would live in White towns as family units for many years, they would be there merely as temporary sojourners, and would be regarded as belonging to some Bantustan or Homeland. Further support to this idea was given by the introduction of the Bantu Homelands Citizenship Bill of 1969. This Bill was not proceeded with because the session was nearing its end. It provides that every African in the Republic who is not a citizen of a self-governing Bantu territory will be a citizen of one or other territorial area. He will, however, remain a citizen of the Republic of South Africa, too, and be accorded protection by the Republic according to international law. But franchise rights will be available to him in his own territory.

Dr. Verwoerd also made it clear that his Nationalist Party supported the policy that the White man should retain his domination over his part of the country and he was prepared to pay a certain price for it – namely, by giving the Bantu full rights to develop in their own areas. Significantly he also stated that if it was within the powers of the Bantu, their territories might develop to full independence, possibly eventually forming a South African Commonwealth with White South Africa serving as its core and as guardian of the emerging Bantu states. The White guardian would meet his obligations on the basis of "creative self-withdrawal".

In 1968, the Transkeian Legislature Assembly passed a motion that the Republican Government be approached to do everything in its power to prepare the Transkei for independence in the shortest possible time. During the same year the Republic's Minister of Bantu Administration and Development made the Government's attitude clear about progress that has to be made before full independence is achieved by the Bantustans. He said his remarks were directed to all Bantustans and not just the Transkei.

The road to full independence, he stated, was a "long

and difficult one". Before any people could aspire to it, certain pre-conditions had to be fulfilled:

1 Considerable administrative experience and control of government departments.
2 Deep-rooted reliability in all actions, particularly in the control of finance and budgeting.
3 Integrity of purpose in public affairs – from the highest to the lowest official.
4 A democratic way of life and a sense of complete responsibility.
5 The control and management of all fields of administration by its own citizens, and not on a large scale by citizens of another country because there were not enough local men qualified to do the work.
6 Economic development and the provision of jobs for its own people by its own government.
7 A firm desire for peaceful co-existence. A nation that wished to govern itself must show by word and deed that it was prepared to live in peace with its own people and with other peoples or nations, especially its neighbours.

Since it is the South African Government that must grant independence to the Homelands the Minister's guidelines for pre-conditions are of special importance. A little study of the conditions makes it clear that independence may not be attained by any of the Homelands except at the wish of the Republican Government and in the very distant future.

At the present moment, for instance, the Transkei has not progressed economically to a stage where it could provide jobs for its own people. There is hardly any Bantustan which would qualify in this condition for the foreseeable future. Again in the Transkei almost all top administrative posts in the government departments are held by Whites, seconded by the Republican Government. Will independence be granted when they have been withdrawn? What happens if a party is elected to govern which is opposed to the Republican Government policy of apartheid?

There can be no doubt, however, that Territorial Authorities themselves are all demanding full independence within the shortest possible time in line with the Transkeian Legislative Assembly's resolution of 1968. In June 1970 Chief Gatsha Buthelezi, the Chairman of the Zulu Territorial Authority, made this important observation on the question of self-government, "We hope that it will not be long before our Territorial Authority is granted more power and before we get full self-government. It is often said that we are not ready for such a step. We challenge such assertions as we Black people of South Africa have had three centuries of contact with your people. Today most African states are governing themselves ... some go through chaos in the process and these are merely growing pains. But there are some that are governing themselves efficiently ... Quite often we enjoy boasting about the fact that we in South Africa have more African graduates than the rest of Africa, how can we therefore dare to think that our own Black people are not good enough to govern themselves?" In the same speech he urged that the policy of Bantustans must be made to work as soon as possible so that it can be proved to be feasible within the shortest possible time. "We cannot be expected to move towards our self-determination and self-realisation at ox wagon pace," he declared.

Now that the Bantu Authorities has been established in all the Homelands what is its future and what is the future of South Africa?

It must be remembered that the Bantu Authorities has been thrust upon the African people by the Government. In his June 1970 speech, Chief Buthelezi stated that "about 1967, officials of the Department of Bantu Administration told some of us that Bantu Affairs Commissioners, who gave us the impression that we had a choice in the matter, 'were wrongly instructed', that we were merely being consulted and that consultation did not mean we have to give consent. Those of us who had been waiting for our people to decide, had, after this explanation, no option but to comply with the law, as the question of accepting or rejecting the Act fell away."

Now that Bantu Authorities has been established in virtually all the Homelands, after twenty years of effort, the question may be asked whether it will now be a permanent feature of South African society. Can the establishment of Bantu Authorities be regarded as the breakthrough on the part of the Government in solving the problem of race relations in South Africa?

The answer to this question is found in the statements of African leaders of Bantu Authorities themselves. Mr. C. Ndamse, a leading member of Chief Matanzima's Cabinet who was at one time banned by Mr. Vorster under the Suppression of Communism Act, is reported to have said of Bantustans that it is better to rule in hell than wash the dishes in heaven!

Chief Buthelezi has said that the people had no choice but to comply with the law in accepting Bantu Authorities. The African people therefore are in Bantu Authorities simply because they feel they have no choice in the matter. Bantu Authorities is part of a philosophy which is repugnant and revolting to anyone who loves justice, fair play and human dignity. It is based on the false assumption that Africans are not entitled to the wealth of South Africa outside the Reserves or Homelands and that they have no rights to land outside these Reserves. Already the leaders of the Territorial Authorities are demanding more land from the Government to accommodate the people who are driven away from White Areas.

Bantustans will not succeed because they are based on a philosophy which seeks to exploit and dominate the majority of the population, for the advantage of the minority.

The Government policies have been challenged by the

African people and their political organisations which were banned in 1960. The struggle for complete equality for all goes on in South Africa under the leadership of the banned African National Congress. Every year the Government passes Draconian laws like the Terrorism Act, the "Boss Law" and laws that provide for indefinite detention, in an attempt to suppress opposition to their policies.

Precisely because of the Republican Government's intransigent attitude towards the granting of political rights to the Africans, the struggle led by the African National Congress has now entered an armed phase – and world opinion has been aroused against the policies of the South African Government.

Bantustans are a passing phase, one of the bad dreams which our people will remember having gone through towards their freedom. One thing must be clear, African people have never accepted Bantu Authorities as an alternative to freedom and democracy in South Africa. It is the duty of all those who love freedom and who are fighting for it to assist our people in the Bantustans to achieve freedom for themselves and for all South Africans.

BARRY OLIVER HIGGS: Born 1943, in Durban, South Africa. He worked in advertising before entering university and was active in student politics and Congress movement. At the age of twenty, he was detained in solitary confinement. In 1964 he left South Africa illegally. Mr. Higgs has worked in Berlin, G.D.R., for *Sechaba*, the A.N.C. magazine and now lives in London. His poetry has been included in several anthologies.

HANDS OFF

Black hands had picked this orange, sent express,
The juice still sparkling in the golden fruit –
While those dry fingers continents away:
Could they still pick, or had they faded out?

For, standing on a barren London street,
I thought: "Black hands have picked this fruit for me.
But a grasping hand has whipped the effort on
And white fists with steel guns guard the tree."

So guilt lay in my hands that day, like blood,
And from the grocer's stall the gruesome load
Of bloody, battered cheaper-by-the-dozen
Dripped bright and dying to the London road.

But no one seemed to notice, hurrying by,
The thousand corpses on the grocer's stall;
Wrapped in the lies of evening fivepence news
The English turned their faces to the wall.

And the innocent greengrocer, hands in his pockets,
Smiling, surrounded by fruit in packets.

J. MAOTO: Born 1938 in South Africa. He received his B.A. in mathematics and psychology at Witwatersrand University. In 1964, he was arrested as co-conspirator in political trial, discharged and placed under house-arrest. Mr. Maoto left South Africa in 1965, and now lives in London.

T. TEMBA: Born 1936 in Newcastle, Natal, South Africa. He left South Africa in 1968; and graduated from the School of Economics, Berlin, G.D.R. Mr. Temba now lives in London.

THE OUTWARD DRIVE
South Africa's Military Machine

The deliberate and systematic militarisation of South African fascism, commencing as it did in the immediate era of decolonisation in Africa, has been escalated inexorably, almost frantically, so that today the Republic possesses a strike potential in terms of arms, military equipment and men which far exceeds the combined strength of all the independent African states south of the Sahara.

It is crucial, particularly within the context of the Southern African conflict, to examine the character and content of those military preparations; the military and political policies which dictate and determine them, and to assess their consequences for Africa generally and Southern Africa in particular.

First a brief examination of the Republic's military preparations and potential.

In the ten year period from 1959–60 onwards, the arms budget has rocketted from R40 million to R271.6 million for 1969–70 (£1 = R 1,714). During the approximately same period the regular defence force (army, navy and air force) has expanded from 7,721 in 1961 to the current 13,200. To this must be added a citizen force (army, navy and air force) of 26,500; a force of 58,000 organised in special units or commandos; the current annual intake of approximately 20,000 conscripts; a 30,000 man police force; a 15,000 man police reserve. In toto, the present armed forces amount to between 200,000 and 250,000 trained men.

Why does the Republic of South Africa find it necessary to mobilise approximately one-third of its male adult population militarily, apart from injecting a war psychosis into White South Africans, and why the necessity to allocate an ever increasing portion of the annual budget to arms and armaments? The answer surely is not merely to cow the forces of national liberation within the country and their allies with a sense of overkill. Indeed the nature of the Republic's armaments, military equipment and development programmes belie such a naive "defence" approach.

The armour possessed by the army is recorded as 100 Centurion tanks and approximately another 100 medium tanks; several hundred armoured cars; an unstated number of scout cars, armoured personnel carriers and light reconnaissance aircraft.

The Republic's air force consists of some 230 aircraft spearheaded by two squadrons of multi-purpose French-built Mirages capable of operating as fighters, bombers, ground-attack or reconnaissance machines, whilst the rest consist of British-manufactured Buccaneer light jet bombers and Canberra long-range bombers; American-built Sabre jet fighters; locally built Italian Impala jet fighters (under licence by Atlas Aircraft Corporation) and French-made Alouette helicopters.

The navy, though less numerically impressive, already comprises 2 destroyers, antisubmarine frigates, helicopter carriers, mine sweepers and 3 French-made deep-diving submarines recently acquired.

With the Security Council Resolution of 1963 imposing a mandatory arms embargo, the Republic embarked on an ambitious programme of armaments self-sufficiency. The dramatic successes achieved, both in tempo and depth, with this programme constitute in fact the most striking indictment of Western power collaboration at all levels.

In 1963 Mr. Fouché, then Minister of Defence, asked the South African White parliament to vote large sums for military research, especially in the missile field. Accordingly in October 1963 Professor le Roux, vice-president of the C.S.I.R. (Council for Scientific and Industrial Research), announced the establishment of the country's own National Institute of Rocket Research to concentrate on ground-to-air missiles. In December 1965 the first missile was successfully fired.

Again in 1963 Professor L. J. le Roux informed a scientific congress in Pretoria that research was being initiated into the virulent gases TABUN, SOMAN and SARIN which are ten times as poisonous as all other known gases; these gases can be sprayed from low flying planes like insecticides and are comparatively cheap to produce.

Need we even ask why this research into poisonous gases? In both these fields – rocket research and poison gases – West German complicity has been elaborately detailed in a memorandum prepared by the Afro-Asian Solidarity Committee entitled "The Bonn-Pretoria Axis".

Nor does the German Federal Republic's involvement

end with these murderous ventures. West-German finance capital is directly allied with the South African state monopolies of ISCOR (Iron and Steel Industrial Corporation), ESCOM (Electricity Supply Commission), I.D.C. (Industrial Development Corporation) and SASOL, the world's largest oil-from-coal plant, and in the construction of the Orange River and Ox-bow hydroelectric schemes.

Despite the Security Council Resolution, M. Fouché was to reveal as early as 1965 that the Republic had obtained 120 licences to manufacture weapons locally and was already practically self-sufficient so far as the production of small weapons, ammunition and explosives were concerned. "We would," he continued, "even be able to sell arms which we manufactured in the country to well-disposed friends."

In 1967 the Atlas Aircraft Corporation began the production of the Italian Impala jet fighter under licence. This factory cost between £15 million and £20 million.

In May 1968 Mr. Botha informed parliament that "numerous" approaches had been made by overseas armaments manufacturers to establish joint firms and introduced in the same year the Armaments Amendment Bill with the object of creating a massive state-owned armaments industry with an initial share capital of nearly £50,000. Thus was created ARMSCOR (Armaments Development and Production Corporation of South Africa) to assist private arms enterprises. Mr. Botha also went on to reveal that development in the electronics field could already provide most of the "defence" force's requirements; that the Republic was already self-sufficient in the manufacture of rifles, mortars, ammunition, aerial bombs, explosives, as well as napalm bombs.

Addressing the South African Air Force Association early in 1969 Mr. Botha was further able to say, "New and modern aircraft and equipment have been acquired, are on order and are included in plans for future orders." In the same year he revealed that in collaboration with a

French electronics firm, South Africa had developed the Cactus air defence system, to date the most effective counter against low-level air attacks.

The Republic is also one of the world's largest producers of uranium and in August 1965 the then Prime Minister, Verwoerd, inaugurated the country's first nuclear reactor, stating, "It is the duty of South Africa not only to consider the military uses of the material, but also to direct its uses to peaceful purposes." (Abdul Minty: South Africa's Defence Strategy, quoting *South African Digest*.) What is sinister in the extreme, however, was the announcement in May 1968 of South Africa's refusal to sign the Nuclear Non-Proliferation Treaty. Botha told the United Nations Political Committee that South Africa would not open her mines for international inspection. Considered in the light of the African states policy of keeping Africa a nuclear free zone, the Republic's posture is indeed ominous.

Such briefly is the militarisation of South Africa. What emerges with irrefutable force and clarity is the degree of complicity, open and devious, of the NATO powers in the past and present, in the building of the South African arsenal. What must be refuted with equal force is the reason so often advanced by the racist regime itself and echoed in circles among the Western Powers (Sir Alec Douglas-Home in Britain) that the arms build-up is solely for defence purposes. The dividing line between offensive and defensive weapons programmes is too superficial for serious consideration, but the reasons for the programmes themselves emerge with great clarity when we consider the politico-economic framework within which they are embarked. It is precisely this which provides the real answers to South Africa's massive arms build-up, determines the position and role adopted and ascribed to the Republic by forces within the country, in Southern Africa and among the Western countries, and underlines the nature of her intentions – aggression –

against both the peoples of Southern Africa fighting racism and Portuguese colonialism, and those independent countries allied with the struggling masses.

The claim that the racist policies and practices of the South African regime constitute a threat not only to the oppressed Black millions within South Africa, but likewise to Southern Africa and the African states north of the Limpopo, has repeatedly been made by the national liberation movement since 1946 when the South African situation was first placed before the UNO General Assembly. That part of this claim has become reality is all the more reason why urgent attention must be given not merely to the policy of racism as it affects the Black majority, but to the real character of the South African state.

The discovery of diamonds in 1865 and gold in 1886 marked the beginnings of the growth of South Africa as the most powerful capitalist state on the African continent, and so dates the growth and power of the South African bourgeoisie.

These discoveries placed South Africa from a poor British colony with little or no investment and remunerative opportunities, to the forefront of the world's investment markets. Capital from abroad, overwhelmingly from imperial Britain, flowed in. Investments in the gold-mining industry increased from R16 million in 1881 to R208 million between 1887 and 1905. S. H. Frakel in Hobart Houghton's book *South African Economy* quotes a figure of R296 million invested in the gold-mining industry of the Witwatersrand alone in 1832. It has been estimated that by 1936 a total of R1,046 million representing approximately 43 per cent of the total foreign investments on the continent of Africa had been poured into South Africa. Due to these discoveries a profound economic revolution took place transforming a patriarchal subsistence economy which has been expanding considerably and continually over the past 100 years. Moreover the last decade has been a period of unparalleled growth.

Between 1960 and 1968 the gross domestic product grew on an average by 6 per cent per annum (compared with the average of approximately 2.5 per cent to 3 per cent for Western Europe). Gold production has continued to rise during the same period by 7 per cent annually; agricultural production by approximately 6 per cent, while the value of manufacturing industry has grown by approximately 11 per cent per year.

Industrial development apart, South Africa's Unit Trust Industry initiated by two companies in 1965, grew to six in 1967. Between 1966 and the end of 1968 their portfolio assets increased from R24.6 million to R400 million, an indication of the growing accumulation of domestic savings which amounts to 24 per cent of the present domestic product.

Yet it would be wholly incorrect to ascribe the development of the South African economy to capital investment only. An essential prerequisite to the exploitation of the mineral riches required the necessity of exploitation of labour. The main labour force is the dispossessed millions of Africans whose resistance to British imperialism and Afrikaner nationalism had only been successfully broken after more than two and a half centuries of bitter fighting. By the turn of the twentieth century the African people had in the main been reduced to a landless, migrant mass – a ready-made source of cheap labour. The Afrikaner people themselves had been crushed after three years of ruthless war by imperial Britain for possession of the rich diamond and gold fields. With the Act of Union in 1910 we witness the wholesale exclusion of the African people from any meaningful participation in the decision and policy-making process of the Union; the exclusion of the majority of Afrikaners from the mainstream of power and economic participation, and the entrenchment of a class willing to oversee what was then largely the interests of the British ruling class.

However, whilst the African majority still remain

powerless economically and politically, the Afrikaners today hold the reins of power, with a growing element within it which holds substantial economic power. In fact the victory of the Nationalist Party in the 1948 elections was a victory of the aspirant Afrikaner capitalist. It is this class within the Afrikaner people which has been militating since 1912, when the Nationalist Party was formed, for political power as a means of attaining economic power. During the twenty-two years of Nationalist government, the share of the Afrikaner capitalist has steadily been increasing. No less than one-quarter of the new millionaires disclosed by the 1967 Stock Exchange listing were Afrikaners.

Whereas in 1948 the defeat of the United Party (the Party of the traditional monopoly capitalists) effectively separated the forces of finance capital, mainly English-speaking, from power and ushered in the era of Afrikaner capitalism, there has been a steady merging of these forces at top levels. This merging of the upper levels of finance – industrial and commercial bourgeoisie – across the economically superficial divisions of Afrikaner and non-Afrikaner has given birth to the Hertzog-led Reconstituted Nationalist Party of *verkramptes* (narrow nationalists). Apart from the ultra-chauvinists in its ranks, the Reconstituted Nationalist Party represents in the main that element amongst the Afrikaner small capitalists who are witnessing their effective exclusion from the league of monopoly capitalism.

But the Republic today is more than an advanced capitalist state. The logical extension of its tremendous economic growth has by the very nature of its internal dynamics necessitated two forms of development, namely, the development of an internal machinery of oppression and repression to keep the Black majority in a permanent state of servitude, and the development of an aggressive expansionist policy to generate capital outside South Africa. The explosive growth in the economy has to be generated outside of the national environment because of the pure economic contradictions of South African racist capitalism. For although the national income has been steadily rising the African majority comprising approximately 70 per cent of the population earn only approximately 19 per cent of the national income.

According to one widely advertised theory capitalist economic development in South Africa will "inevitably" lead to "liberalisation" of the regime. The April 1970 issue of *African Affairs* however published a remarkable article entitled "White Supremacy and White Prosperity in South Africa Today" by Frederick Johnstone of Oxford. He proceeds to show that "far from undermining white supremacy, economic development is constantly reinforcing it. Its power structure is continually strengthened by its own material output. In a circular process, the African workers produce the wealth and power which enable the whites to go on strengthening this structure of production which goes on producing power which goes on strengthening the structure and so on. It is precisely the function of actual apartheid to render this process as effective as possible."

Not only has there been a considerable accumulation of capital reserves, but the most dramatic change in the economic development of South Africa in the manufacturing industry is accentuating the basic contradiction and makes the demand for alternative outlets an urgent necessity. Although the mining industries in gold and diamonds have been and will be for the next 50 years or so, the largest single source of foreign earnings, the need for diversifying has been seen as a priority measure for a long time. Thus the growth of the manufacturing industry has risen from a gross output of approximately R32 million in 1924-25 to R1,400 million in 1965.

It is this major contradiction in the economic field which has necessitated a shift in the political posture of the Republic – from Verwoerd's *verkramptes* or isolationist policy to Vorster's so-called *verligtes* blandly aggressive and expansionist policy. The triumph of capital over ideology, and confirmation of the inexorable law of capital – expand or bust.

Southern Africa and Africa north of the Limpopo represents the most convenient market for the Republic's economic penetration. Trade figures, capital investments and military involvement in Africa already confirm and testify to the New Deal of the Vorster regime. Whilst the bulk of the Republic's exports to the industrially developed Western countries consist mainly of primary goods and only 6 per cent manufactured goods, 75 per cent of the trade with the African states and the under-developed countries, consists of manufactured goods.

In a very real sense therefore the Republic exhibits all the features of an imperialist power with a powerful ruling class channelling its own interests through fascist organs with vast interests in the Republic itself; in South West Africa which it has forcibly annexed despite the U.N. resolution of 1966 terminating her mandate; in Zimbabwe where it is now the dominant partner as a result of the U.D.I. exceeding even British and American capital interest; in Angola where it is involved in partnership with the Portuguese, West German, British and American capital in exploiting mineral and oil deposits; in Mozambique where it is part of the international capitalist consortium constructing the Cabora Bassa Dam; in the former High Commission territories of Lesotho, Botswana and Swaziland; in Malawi where Banda, apart from openly supporting its aggressive military designs against the liberation movements, has given it senior rights to investment; in Katanga and Congo (K) where it is in alliance with the international finance group of Union Minière. And to a limited degree in the capitalist countries themselves.

The chief features of an imperialist state are being accelerated. During the period 1964-1969, for example, over three hundred mergers took place (*The Times*, 27 October 1969), while the movement towards monopoly capitalism is characterised by the extension of the holdings of the seven mining-finance houses headed by the Anglo-American Corporation with assets over R2,500 million, in many areas of the economy. This domestic scene apart, there has also been a merging of international capital with South African imperialism, through the process of interlocking directorships and holdings in companies that are supranational, e.g. Union Minière.

A proper assessment therefore of the Republic's arms build-up must recognise the fact of South African imperialism as a force which is not only concerned with the maintenance of racism and fascism internally, but needs to safeguard the economic interests of the South African ruling class and its allies in the Western countries. Not only that but it needs to neutralise effectively the opposition of the independent African states, strengthen the Portuguese colonialists and the U.D.I. regime in Zimbabwe militarily and economically as an insurance policy against the success of the national liberation movements and the consequent destruction of the White power structure in Southern Africa. Hence the Republic's military involvement in Zimbabwe, Angola and Mozambique. Hence the Republic's economic backing for the Smith regime and the grand design of the Cabora Bassa Dam, which apart from its immediate economic benefits, is a political means of insulating the Republic against the downward sweep of the forces of freedom.

In the light of the above analysis, and having due regard for the character of the armaments programme, let us examine once more the Republic's arms build-up and the usual reasons advanced for it both by the government of South Africa as well as its many allies amongst the NATO countries.

First it has been claimed that the military preparations are necessary and vital for the Republic's very existence because of the imminent threat and possibility of aggression from independent African states. This argument is ridiculous if one considers the balance of armed forces between South Africa and the African states. Individually or united, none of the African states is powerful enough to lend any sustenance to ambitions, legitimate for Africa, to overthrow the apartheid state. Nor has any African state ever threatened to invade the Republic or instituted developments within their programme that can be construed as preparations for military aggression. Indeed it has been the Republic which has threatened to strike at the countries lending support to the liberation movements. Both Tanzania and Zambia have been bitterly criticised and attacked for their active support of the freedom movements, and threats of pre-emptive strikes against them have become a regular feature of the Republic's attitude to these countries.

Secondly, the government of the Republic has repeatedly argued that the military preparations are a necessary contribution to the NATO countries. Spokesmen in the U.S.A. and Britain have at various times supported the claim that certain strategic interests exist between the NATO countries and South Africa. This point is not argued since the "strategic interests" referred to are precisely in the enormous economic stakes of the Western powers in Africa and Southern Africa. But the Republic's contribution in terms of balance of world armaments cannot make the slightest impression. The only real sense that this "contribution" can make is as a force for aggression and counter-revolution in Africa, as a check against real social and economic progress and a guarantee for maintaining White supremacy and superprofits. Behind the forces of local reaction stands the might of the great imperialist powers: Great Britain, the U.S.A., France, West Germany and Japan. White supremacist and colonialist rule in Southern Africa is in direct alliance with and an integral part of international imperialism. There may be internal conflicts and embarrassments, but against the forces of progress, reaction stands united.

One of the key factors that goes a long way to explain the Western powers' continued complicity in arming to the teeth White Supremacy and Portuguese colonialism, is to be found in the twin realities of their huge economic stakes in Southern Africa and the breakup of their formal colonial empires by the sweep of African independence.

In particular this applies to Great Britain. The apartheid policy is a source of huge profits because of the ruthless economic exploitation of the African majority. A low cost economy with a higher capital investment yield than that offered anywhere else is worth maintaining and arming. For this reservoir to continue, investments and national exploitation based on race must also continue. It can only continue in the teeth of the fierce struggles for freedom conducted by the oppressed majority; it can only be maintained by systematic terror and violence. Western power stakes in the Republic and Southern Africa are considerable – something of the order of £2,000 million sterling, with more than half being British capital investment, and increasing steadily by £50 to £100 million a year. U.S. stakes are the second largest and certainly larger than elsewhere on the continent. The rate of capital investment is being steadily increased by all Western powers – Britain, the U.S.A., France and West Germany with Japan as the latest newcomer. Based around the mining and finance houses in South Africa, giant international cartels are involved in the Southern African complex.

For the former colonial powers, especially Great Britain, South Africa, apart from providing a base through which to channel their economic interests, serves as a viable aggressive presence south of the Sahara.

"When we take exception to the increasing foreign investment in South Africa, we do so not because we are opposed to investments as such, but because investments in South Africa strengthens the hands of the racists. For all practical purposes, therefore, foreign interests are collaborators with the fascist South African regime and partners in racial discrimination. More than that, they help to strengthen its military power, for, according to the elementary laws of economics, investment is profitable only in countries offering a guarantee of stability. An unholy alliance has therefore been formed by South Africa's major trading partners with the object of keeping Southern Africa under permanent tutelage."

This statement, made by Mr. A. Marof, Guinea's ambassador to the United Nations and member of the U.N. Special Committee on Apartheid, reflects the oft-repeated emphasis made by opponents of racism.

Bibliography

Survey of Race Relations 1969, S. A. Institute of Race Relations.
South African Arms Strategy, Abdul Minty.
Special Bulletin on S. A. Defence Strategy, issued by South Africa House, London.
South African Economy, Hobart Houghton, University Press, Cape Town.
South African Communist, 3rd Quarter 1967.
The Bonn-Pretoria Axis, Afro-Asian Solidarity Committee.

BREYTEN BREYTENBACH: Born 1939 in Bonnievale, Cape Province, South Africa, left his country in 1959 to live in Paris. For several years he was refused permission to visit South Africa with his wife who is Vietnamese, i. e. not white. Later the restriction was lifted. When visiting South Africa once more in 1976, Breytenbach was arrested for subversive activities against the state and sentenced to nine years imprisonment. Statements made during his trial and subsequently, indicate that he no longer holds the views expressed here.

VULTURE CULTURE
The Alienation of White South Africa

It is my contention that the culture of the White people in South Africa is an organic development of "Western civilisation". It may be a perversion thereof, it may crystallise only certain elements of that civilisation and omit others which, at a pinch, might have softened the features — but surely this crudeness is due to their being cultural settlers. White South Africa is Western and Christian just as French Algeria and British Kenya were, just as Alabama and the Vietnam war are; it is as Western and as Christian as large sectors of the Western world's population would want them to remain or to become.

Looking into South Africa is like looking into the mirror at midnight when one has pulled a face and a train blew its whistle and one's image stayed there, fixed for all eternity. A horrible face, but one's own.

Apartheid is the state and the condition of being apart. It is the no man's land between peoples. But this gap is not a neutral space. It is the artificially created distance necessary to attenuate, for the practitioners, the very raw reality of racial, economic, social and cultural discrimination and exploitation. It is the space of the White man's being. It is the distance needed to convince himself of his denial of the other's humanity. It ends up denying all humanity of any kind both to the other and to himself.

Apartheid is the White man's night, the darkness which blurs his consciousness and his conscience. What one doesn't see doesn't exist. Also, at night one doesn't balk at the skin deep peculiarities of the girl you sleep with. They are all pink on the inside.

But that which may be a psychic purge for the White (his binoculars to see the end of his nose with), is a physical straining for the Black; the confines and the confinement of his condition, the maiming of his possibilities. White is the Black man's burden and what he wishes for most, probably, is for the man to get off his bloody back and stand on his own two feet.

Apartheid is at the same time the implement of exploitation and the implementation thereof. It is the lion tamer's whip and stool. The lion sees stool, whip and man as one.

Obviously, this instrument of repression is also used, structurally, on White society itself. In the name of the State – the State is the daughter of apartheid – all dissidence is suppressed. White workers too are told to sacrifice their legitimate claims on behalf of apartheid.

It is fascist. ("Fascism: the principles and organisation

of the patriotic and anti-communist movement . . ." of *The Concise Oxford Dictionary*.)

It is totalitarian. ("Totalitarian: relating to a policy that permits no rival loyalties or parties.")

Apartheid is alienation – estrangement leading towards insanity.

It is schizophrenic – a mental disease marked by disconnection between thoughts, feelings and actions.

It is paranoic – mental derangement, especially when marked by delusions of grandeur, persecution, etc.

For the White man, apartheid is a distance of mind, a state of being, the state of apartness. From the assumption of apartness – from the necessity to stress this apartness, to justify and rationalise it, to obscure that which may strip him naked – White culture in South Africa is born.

Apartheid is White culture.

What is culture?

In a UNESCO publication, *Cultural Rights as Human Rights,* it says: "Culture is a process of communication between men; it is the essence of being human." It states further that this communication can only take place effectively when the poor throughout the world are liberated from poverty, disease and illiteracy.

And in the same publication Francis Jeanson puts it this way: "Culture is the perpetual creation of values which are born only to be superseded . . . A cultural act is, in the last resort, a solemn and even risky decision implying a total engagement of the individual conscience concerned . . . I would add that this amounts to a venture, in the best sense of the word, aimed at arousing in people a profound political consciousness . . . (It) is a venture which is based on a refusal: the refusal to accept a certain exclusion, a certain alienation. This by no means implies any attempt to camouflage the economic causes of such an exclusion; but these must be fought with political weapons."

"The community must be returned to itself." – George Lamming.

The culture of the Whites in Saint Albino – this state of whiteness, the prison of laws and taboos – negates all political consciousness. Apartheid justifies itself in the name of Western civilisation, in the name of the Afrikaans culture. The tendency is there sometimes to think that apartheid is an unpopular dogmatism devised by a few bureaucrats and some perverted theoreticians and imposed (also) on the majority of Afrikaners. One must point out that the Afrikaners are responsible for apartheid, collectively and individually. Without them it would not exist. It is their way of life. If the Whites as individuals, if all those who practise culture (the intellectuals, the academics, the artists, the authors, etc.) were to withdraw their direct or implied support of apartheid – not only of a particular government, but of the ethics of Albino-hood itself – it could not last.

In their thrust for power the Afrikaners defined themselves as a cultural entity. They still propagate this defensive definition of themselves with vehemence and passion. Given their origins one can understand the passion. They are descendants of emigrants who were forced out of Europe or were ill-adapted to it – sailors, mercenaries, down-graded civil servants – and difficult minorities such as the Huguenots whom the Dutch authorities farmed out to their African colony. (Europe has always shown the tendency to solve its ethnic, religious and social problems by offloading the unassimilables onto the Third World.) Locally non-European blood was mixed in: the blood of slaves, the blood of the conquered ones. Neglected, unsupported and unprotected by the motherlands – until diamonds and gold were found – they soon imposed, in the first place upon themselves, their view of what they thought themselves forced to be: a new "people", still White; an extension of European culture – which meant Calvinist puritanism – into hostile but covetable surroundings. Thus we have from the very outset insecurity and a correspondingly passionate affirmation of the nature and principles of the tribe. Doubt will be suppressed, purity must be preserved, descendence is to be whitewashed and there results a pathetic clinging to "European" culture. (It is the story of the pale virgin with the dark-skinned brood.) One pretends to be what you are told you ought to be. Naturally this identification could only be – can only be – with the outward and fossilised signs of European ways.

Consequently we find a literature which does not issue from personal experience, but is grafted onto another, European literature; art grows out of art; culture is a parody of Europe's cultures; aesthetics are unrelated to any conceivable facet of reality. Culturally Saint Albino Whites live from overseas offal. (Spiced it is true, with what can be taken from indigenous cultures – as in the field of popular music for instance.)

Thus we can see that in the beginning there was uncertainty, ignorance and greed. Therefore fear and the need to define. The definition was based simplistically on the aspects which most obviously marked the settlers as different from those around them. This definition (White, European, Protestant) allowed for greed to be rationalised as survival at first; later as independence and guidance and civilisation and justice. And culture. The tribe became a power. If you say power you also say Party or Church, and the Party must have priests to protect its Whiteness. But this purity is based on a lie. Yet, the purity must not be questioned. Only, truth is awareness which needs to extend its grasp to survive. Therefore: dichotomy. The tribe's power is to the advantage – in the first place – of the bourgeoisie; they prefer the norm to the truth and they see to it that the priests affirm and reaffirm this norm. The tribe becomes a closed fist. Now there is ossification of attitudes, ultimately even contraction cramping the fingers and cutting off all the blood flow. There is withdrawal into the unpolluted air inside the cramped fist. In the last stage gangrene sets in. And in any case – uncertainty, ignorance and greed. Therefore fear and the need to define.

The tribal ethos of the Afrikaners consists of negation, suppression, withdrawal and reaction.

What, more precisely, are the effects of apartheid on White South African culture?

The first thing to point out is that apartheid works. It may not function administratively, its justifications and claims are absurd and it certainly has not succeeded in dehumanising – entirely – the Africans, the Coloureds or the Indians. *But it has effectively managed to isolate the White man.* He is becoming conditioned by his lack of contact with the people of the country, his lack of contact with the South African inside himself. Even though he has become a mental Special Branch, a BOSS of darkness, he doesn't know what's going on – since he can only relate to the syndrome of his isolation. His windows are painted white to keep the night in.

For the White author or artist it results in less contact with reality. He cannot dare look into himself. He doesn't wish to be bothered with his responsibilities as a member of the "chosen" and dominating group. He withdraws and longs for the tranquillity of a little intellectual house on the plain by a transparent river. He will consider himself a new "realist", an "anti-idealist". "This is the way it is," he says. "It has always been a horrible world to live in. This is the way I am. I just want to be an ordinary human being, free to write or paint or film as I wish. I don't want to have anything to do with dirty politics." He cannot identify with anyone but his colleagues, any other class but his own White well-to-do one, and with this he probably identifies by default. His culture is used to shield him from an experience, or even an approximation, of the reality of injustices.

A prominent young *Sestiger* (a *Sestiger* is a youngish Afrikaner who kicked up his heels a bit during the 'sixties) when asked what he thought about the many books banned in the country, wrote: "... Once we've learned to think independently and responsibly, many of my English colleagues will no longer write books that have to be banned."

How can the White man *feel* angry about his injustice which doesn't *affect* him – that is, whose effects he refuses to recognise?

But even so he feels the need, natural to the intellectual, to contest and criticise. Since the "fight for survival" of the tribe was made in the name of its culture – its language and religion – the Poet-Thinker has always played a very important role. The tribe expects the Poet to be an exponent of its tribal values, not a dissenter. These values are power values only, and at times the Poet knows this. He knows that whatever is published is on sufferance of the Publications Board. The establishment will spare no effort to prevent the publication of a work which may play into the hands of the "enemy" – the enemy being the people of South Africa. But this suppression, if it concerns work by an Afrikaner – the offensive work in English is simply banned – will be subtle, or at least discreet and out of public sight, for the sake of the façade of tribal unity. Invariably it will take place before publication.

How? Through the classical carrot-and-stick approach. The carrot is the possibility of having the book prescribed for schools or bought in bulk by provincial libraries; of being commissioned to write or translate for one of the provincial theatre councils; the carrot is any of a number of literary prizes; of being taken to the bosom of the tribe by being put on a pedestal – of becoming the Poet.

The stick can be the spelling out (beforehand) of any of a whole series of laws: the law on blasphemy, the law protecting any section of the population against verbal injury, the law on the suppression of communism, even the law against terrorism. (I need not remind you that these are some of the walls of apartheid.) Or senior intellectuals when consulted in their capacity as guardians of the

Culture will advise against unnecessary and disruptive controversy: "high instances" will pick up the phone to enquire, to threaten or even to bargain; a member of the Publications Board (who may also be a respected *literatum doctor* or a writer) will intervene (beforehand) to confirm in private. If all else fails the printers will simply refuse to print the objectionable work.

The Poet is scolded and cajoled; he hears of the considered opinions of publishers' lawyers; he learns that the publishers simply cannot afford the financial strain of being sued by the State etc. So the Poet sets about changing words; he cuts lines and deletes poems; he cleanses titles and forgets about certain books. The next time around he will cut before sending the work off. And presumably he won't bother to write unacceptable things after that. For the Poet cringes. He cringes before the possibility of being kicked out of the tribe, of thus losing his "identity" and his "relevance". He attempts to reduce the area of possible friction between him and the tribe and – with eyes closed – he invariably starts writing *right*. And now he is cringing before the Word, or – to be less dramatic – before his conscience. In this way our Poet becomes the tongue of the tribe – but not by telling them what they refuse to listen to.

Note that there is no legal precedent which can give weight to the considerations used to pressurise the author; he is convinced solely by the lawyers' interpretations of the law in question. No Afrikaans book has yet been prosecuted. What other evidence can indicate more eloquently the rot to which the Afrikaner intellectuals (and their publishers and teachers) have succumbed?

And to soothe his ego he will, as an enlightened one, push forward and attack certain taboos, as taboos. Thus for example the fight against the restrictions on the presentation of sensuality. Thus, too, forms of racial discrimination are attacked as a taboo would be – to shock and excite the attention of the tribe. It is not the reality of discrimination which is attacked, nor its implications, since that would lead into uncontrollable darkness. If one were to start unravelling all that thread you'll soon find yourself with no clothes at all; you'd have to envisage the destruction of the tribe of the Afrikaner as an Afrikaner, for discrimination is embedded in the tribe, is the *sine qua non* of its existence.

And these attacks are so much grist for the mill of apartheid. "Stinging denunciations, the exposing of distressing conditions and passions which find their outlet in expression are in fact assimilated by the occupying power in a cathartic process. To aid such processes is in a certain sense to avoid their dramatisation and to clear the atmosphere." – Fanon.

I have tried to show how the culture of the Whites in South Africa is at present a framework of lies and compromise – and that it therefore leads to dishonesty, corruption, degradation, shame and decay. The tone, the climate of the creative artist's environment is the system of institutionalised violence. Although this violence is seldom directed against him he still has to live in the system – in fact, he is part of that system. The White artist no longer denounces this violence – the hangings, the shootings, the beatings, the torture in prisons, the horror of "transit camps", the "clearing up of black spots", or the slower and more insidious violence of poverty and undernourishment and disease and infant mortality and the pass system and the daily harassment ... Apartheid allows him to be blind to this and if you tell him he will not believe you, he will accuse you of exaggeration for subversive political purposes. He is part of the bulwark against the dark forces of chaos, anarchy, communism. In the developing revolutionary struggle in the country the people will be even more polarised. During the time before complete liberation can be won the White man's isolation will deepen. We must expect White cultural spokesmen to become even less sensitive to atrocities perpetrated by their government; yet, paradoxically, their hypersensitivity and touchiness will increase with the growing challenge to their comfortable and comforting assumptions.

The White man has become brutalised. He can permit himself to reason away brutality. And in due course his sensitivity becomes blunted. Man lives through and in man. The writer, the artist who closes his eyes to everyday injustice and inhumanity will without fail see less with his writing or painting eyes too. His work will become barren. When one prefers not to see certain things, when one chooses not to hear certain voices, when one's tongue is used only to justify this choice – then the things one turned away from do not cease to exist, the voices do not stop shouting, but one's eyes become walled, one's ears less sensitive, therefore deaf, one's tongue will make some decadent clacking noises and one's hands will only be groping over oneself.

Although the White artist may pretend to be unassailable behind the arrogant walls of his isolation – "Why should I go to visit Black writers," a young Afrikaner intellectual told me, "when they don't take the trouble of visiting me?" – his work will be bedevilled by insecurity and a complex of inferiority. Outside the walls of his prison he will sense the disapproval and the ostracism.

These corrosive effects are clear in the works themselves. One finds that manifestations of culture – from, for and by the Whites – in South Africa are hidebound by traditionalism, a sentimentalised traditionalism. When you believe what you want to believe, you are a sentimentalist. In this genre one will come across the glorification of simple values, of earthy and patriotic atmospheres. This work, it is felt, gives some mental stability because it speaks of eternal truths. One is reminded by nothing as much as by the works written and painted during Hitler's reign – though the technical ability may perhaps not be of the same order.

The alternative to the above is a frenzied experimentalism with the forms of the arts; it is a wallowing in the cerebral and the abstract and avoiding any content that might commit one to a view of human relationships. It is the all out effort to keep the hands clean. Whatever the form the cultural expression finds, it tends to simplify and alienate the subjects treated. White South African culture is describing, not participatory.

When one is not equipped with the faculties which will allow you to integrate and participate – for to integrate you must be able to *move*, then the "knowledge" of yourself and others and phenomena and objects around you becomes very important. "Understanding" is in that sense a limitation which you impose on all these unknowns. What is more, you have to impose these limitations quickly, you have to tie them down with definitions, before they flaunt their dark natures at you in some disgusting – because unknown and untyped – way. To do this, you yourself and all around you must be reasonably static. How else are you going to be orientated? And so you simplify and cut right down to the image of the outer garments. The protection of one's purity implies the straining of one's surroundings through a simplifying eye.

We must not make the mistake of assuming that serious differences exist between the establishment and its cultural exponents. The establishment could not exist without its elite and *vice versa*. They are in the continuous process of creating one another. They are in fact the same people: the power structure.

The totalitarian regime existing in a hostile environment must draw the noose within which it protects itself from contamination ever tighter; it must continue to create new and more abominable laws, it must constantly redefine purity or its cultural values – closely identified with its politics – are strangled.

If you write or paint or film as an Afrikaner you have to compromise the only raw material you have, yourself, your own integrity. You become alienated from yourself which is worse than being cut off from the tribe. You become a hack. The fine intelligence you may have possessed becomes a raw wound; you deaden your insides with money or with editing – and then you are immured into the façade you may once have thought of cracking. You are now stinking while still on your feet. And in turn you become fodder for the tribe, you become part of the pressure which will be brought to bear upon fools more audacious than you can permit yourself to be. Because your corruption must be seen as having a necessary and pragmatic adaptation to *the reality of South Africa.*

The South African authorities have nothing to fear from its intelligentsia. The boys are good and they will improve as they outgrow this infantile need to rebel.

But the reality of South Africa is not theirs; the future of the country is in the hands of all its people. There is no other fight for culture that can develop apart from the popular struggle. The cultural death wish of the "representatives of Western culture" will make them the strings on Nero's fiddle.

DENNIS BRUTUS: Born 1924, in Rhodesia of South African parents; educated at Fort Hare University College, Cape. He was a teacher in Port Elizabeth for 14 years and has been active against apartheid in education and sport. In 1961, he was banned from teaching, writing and organisations. Arrested in 1963 for attending sport meetings, and sentenced to 18 months hard-labour on Robben Island Prison. After release, placed under house-arrest. He now lives in London with his family. Mr. Brutus is president of the South African Non-Racial Open Committee (SAN-ROC) for sport; and on the staff of the International Defence and Aid Fund. He has published two volumes of poetry, *Sirens, Knuckles, Boots* and *Letters to Martha*.

THE SPORTSMAN'S CHOICE

Apartheid South Africa is accepted by a large part of the world as one of the perennial problems of our time – widely and generally condemned, but without much expectation of change; and so the press treats it as a rather tedious subject, with little that is fresh, and the man in the street feels that little can be done about it.

But there is one aspect of the apartheid policy which frequently gets into the news, and where it seems, not only that things are happening, but they are actually bringing about some changes in a rather tiresome scene.

This is sport, which has regularly, for some years, been

debated and disputed in various parts of the world, and for a time captured the headlines in Britain, in the course of a South African rugby tour and an aborted cricket tour. And there were other sports events, including South Africa's exclusion from the Olympic movement and suspension from world athletics, which attract international attention.

All this has been interesting, not only because this was an issue in which the common man had an interest (sport has become a universal phenomenon in all societies and often a means of securing national prestige) but because it was an area in which protest against apartheid, which so often seemed futile and ineffective, had actually made some real gains.

The significance of the advance of sport goes deeper than that.

To understand its importance it is necessary to recall that South Africa is, by general agreement, the most sports-mad country in the world; to realise that the vast majority of the 19 million population and certainly almost the entire 3 million Whites in the society have an obsessive interest in sport; and that the matter of policy in sport is so central to the whole politics of the country that it was a disagreement in sport with a Cabinet Minister and his followers which forced the Prime Minister, Mr. Balthazar Vorster, to call a General Election a year before it was due.

Why sport should be of such vital importance to South Africa is difficult to say. But certain factors can be adduced. One is the splendid climate all the year round, which makes it possible for so much outdoor activity to be engaged in; another is the abundance of open space; another is the poverty of cultural life, so that there are few other pursuits to distract. In addition, the distinguished record of South African sportsmen (Gary Player in golf, and Karen Muir in swimming and Paul Nash in athletics) as well as the achievements of the country in team sports. While glories of victory on the sports fields contrive to reassure White South Africans of their worth, and to allow them to crow over those who condemn them. For a country largely cut off from the cultural contact with other countries and subject to world-wide condemnation of its policies, sport has become the great link, as well as the great means by which the national psyche can find compensation.

For someone not familiar with the South African scene, it is not easy to grasp the extent to which sport dominates the thinking of most South Africans. Perhaps the most graphic demonstration of this is the extent and the frequency of sports issues appearing in the headlines of most of the daily newspapers – disasters and international affairs elsewhere are mere trifles compared to a rugby victory or even anticipation of a victory!

Sport is, of course, woven into the fabric of the apartheid society – and is determined by it. It may well be that those in other countries who object to protests being directed at South African sportsmen are simply not aware of how completely all South African sport is directed by the apartheid policy. They tend to assume that it is sport pretty much as it is played elsewhere in the world. But in fact all sport is run on rigid racial lines, and it was because he understood how essential it was that apartheid sport should be preserved that the late Dr. Verwoerd made his famous Loskop Dam speech. Speaking of the inclusion of the Maoris in the New Zealand rugby team to South Africa, he declared that if a single Maori was permitted to be a member of the team it would be sufficient to sabotage the entire structure of the South African society.

But things have changed in some measure since then. Under Mr. Vorster and in the face of the opposition from his rebels who formed their own party, he has since allowed a New Zealand touring team to play in South Africa which included Maoris – and a Samoan.

How has this change come about? It is in fact the direct

result of persistent pressure, both from South Africans and the world, who have stood resolutely against the intrusion of racialism into an area to which it can have no pretence of belonging, that of sport.

Before dealing with this aspect, it would be useful to sketch briefly the structure of South African sport and to indicate the extent to which it is ruled by apartheid.

All sport in South Africa is apartheid sport. There is sport for White South Africans and sport for the non-Whites – whether they are Africans or Coloureds (mixed descent) or Asians. And no non-White may ever join a sports body for Whites. For the Whites there are all the privileges of their White aristocracy – excellent fields and facilities, ample finances and massive press coverage. For the non-Whites there is confinement to inadequate areas in their ghettos or "locations" – often no more than a badly surfaced open area outside the township (though there are one or two show places for visitors, chiefly provided for the miners in their compounds by the large mining corporations and limited to these). In addition, they have all the difficulties associated with being badly paid, exploited and overworked, and denied the training facilities and diet which are needed for development in sport.

All the national South African sports bodies are open only to the White fifth of the nation, and for a non-White to enter a swimming pool, or play on a field reserved for the White population would lead to arrest and imprisonment. Even those non-Whites who simply dare to speak critically about the system are likely to suffer the attention of the Secret Police.

What makes South Africa unique is that this policy was publicly declared, and is legislated for in Acts such as the Group Areas Act at the same time that South Africa seeks to retain membership of the Olympic movement and the international bodies which control world sport in each specific code of sport whose constitutions explicitly declare, as the Charter of the International Olympic Committee does, that *there shall be no discrimination on the grounds of race, religion or politics.*

The battle therefore has been either to secure observance by South Africa of the international constitutions or to ensure that the world bodies should take action against one of their members who openly violates the constitution. It has been a long and surprisingly hard battle – chiefly because the Western countries who often have a preponderance of votes on the world bodies have shown themselves to be staunch friends of apartheid South Africa and have done everything in their power to block action.

But the successes chalked up over the years have been considerable. Though there have been racial divisions in South Africa sport since the Union of South Africa was established in 1910, and progress was at first extremely slow, by 1970 action has been taken in a number of sports resulting in either expulsion or suspension of South Africa from the following international sports bodies: athletics, angling, boxing, basketball, badminton, canoeing, fencing, gymnastics, judo, netball, pentathlon, soccer, tennis, table tennis, weight-lifting, and wrestling. This leaves only a few minor sports – baseball and softball are played on a very small scale – of those in the Olympic ambit. Both rugby and cricket have been under considerable pressure – notably with the cancellation of the cricket tour in Britain 1970, and these are sports where pressure will continue to develop. The beginnings of the protest movement in sport were in South Africa and were so small that they were for long dismissed as insignificant foolishness. But the movement has since grown to international dimensions (in Norway, Sweden, Denmark and Holland, both German States and Britain, in New Zealand, Australia and the United States) so that it has now become a powerful international force which has achieved considerable success. The pressures organised at the time of the Mexico Olympics in 1968 were the greatest: a massive build-up of pressures by sporting bodies throughout the world which led to the threat of more than forty-six countries boycotting the Olympics if the South Africans took part. This was the real reason for the decision by an emergency meeting of the executive of the I.O.C. (the International Olympic Committee) to withdraw the invitation issued to South Africa.

One aspect of the 1968 debate is often misrepresented and so it may be useful to clear it up here. It is often said that South Africa had undertaken to send, for the first time, a truly representative team which would be chosen on merit and which would include non-Whites. This is not the whole truth. There are documents to show that the offer made by the South African Olympic Committee was in fact a conditional one – that only those non-Whites who were prepared to accept apartheid in sport would be considered for selection. It was this condition that caused the majority of the non-White sportsmen to reject the offer, and it was the knowledge of this that enabled the General Clerk, President of the Mexican Olympic Committee, to decline to follow the order of the I.O.C. that he should issue an invitation to South Africa.

The beginnings: because the non-Whites were excluded from the national sports bodies, they tended to set up their own organisations – first regional and then national. They too tended at first to have racial divisions among themselves, mainly because they were separated and found themselves in pockets throughout the country. But they became increasingly aware of the requirements of the world bodies – that racialism was forbidden, and sought to eliminate racial clauses from the constitutions. At the same time they became conscious of the anomaly – the national bodies of their country were not only non-national, but they were also guilty of contravening the statutes which forbade racial discrimination. Perhaps the most important factor was the emergence of some sportsmen of very high standard – people who could have qualified for the national representative teams if it were not for their colour. From this came the determination to seek recognition for their sportsmen from the national bodies, and failing that, through appeal to the international bodies governing world sport for a particular code.

Thus in the late 'forties and early 'fifties, efforts were made to secure recognition in various sports, including soccer, table tennis and weight-lifting.

Success came fairly early for table tennis – it was a new body and had some liberal officials, so that now the non-racial body is a full member of the I.T.T.F. and the exclusively White body is excluded from membership. But all of them had much the same experience. On application to the world body they were told that this was a matter for the International Olympic Committee and then on application to the I.O.C. they were told that this was a matter for the South African Olympic Committee. This body recognised, when approached, that its affiliates, the various sports bodies had racially exclusive constitutions but explained that it was powerless to act – either because it was "tradition" to have a racial policy, or, later, because it was the law of the land – citing Acts such as the Riotous Assemblies Act or the Group Areas Act.

It was this failure of the separate sports bodies to make headway which led to the realisation that it was necessary to co-ordinate their efforts. The first effort, the C.C.I.R.S. (Co-ordinating Committee for International Recognition of Sport) failed for lack of support. Many sportsmen were timid and unsure of the powers of the police. But the later S.A.S.A. (South African Sports Association) set up in 1958 prospered and gained increasing strength, particularly when it successfully led opposition to a tour by an all-Black cricket team – a ruse to protect the White cricket body from protest at the meetings of the International Cricket Conference. But S.A.S.A. was unable to crack the solid opposition of the supreme body for sport in South Africa – the South African Olympic Committee – and so was forced into creating a direct challenge to the Olympic

Committee, which did not conceal its support for rascism in sport, by setting up a rival body – SAN-ROC – the South African Non-Racial Olympic Committee.

SAN-ROC had a relatively short run in South Africa. The President was banned from membership of any sports body, attending any sports meeting and sent to prison. The acting chairman, who subsequently became involved in underground sabotage activities, was convicted of causing an explosion and hanged. The other members of the Committee were intimidated or hounded by the police so that some fled the country and others were forced to withdraw from activities.

But SAN-ROC had a considerable impact and to it must be credited the first major success – the exclusion of the country from the Olympics at Tokyo in 1964.

SAN-ROC took on a fresh lease of life in Britain in 1966 where some members of the Committee revived the body, were joined by the President, now exiled from South Africa, and generously assisted by Christian Action and the International Defence and Aid Fund of Canon John Collins, began to campaign vigorously.

Because only the White bodies from South Africa were recognised as members of the international sports bodies, SAN-ROC had no official standing at international congresses, but it was able to do a great deal by way of lobbying and preparation of memoranda and documents which were made available to delegates attending these congresses. Above all, the ability to make personal contact and to answer queries of delegates who, however sympathetic they might be, had only a vague idea of the true position and were able to contradict the false arguments advanced by the South African delegates and their allies – this was a decisive factor and one which was made possible through the generous and enthusiastic support of Canon John Collins and his Defence and Aid Fund. Thus spokesmen from SAN-ROC were to be seen at most of the annual congresses of international sports bodies at which the race question was discussed, including Basle, Budapest, Bamako, Dortmund, Rome, Amsterdam, Warsaw, Dubrovnik, London, Mexico, Teheran, Grenoble, Lagos, Lausanne, and Brazzaville.

Among these was one of the most important at Bamako, Mali – the inaugural meeting of the Supreme Council for Sport in Africa. At this gathering of the nations of Africa, the broad strategy for the African sports bodies in relation to racism in sport and specifically the South African question was defined. It was this agreement that led to the most impressive demonstration of cohesion and unified pressure by the African countries ever seen which, after it had enlisted the support of other countries in Asia, Europe and America, led to the great success at Mexico, when the I.O.C. was forced to exclude South Africa.

In this context, it would be churlish to fail to mention the strong and steady support the African countries enjoyed from the Socialist countries, not only in the Olympics, but also in the particular codes of sport, with the Soviet Union, Hungary, Poland, and Yugoslavia playing a significant part. But other European countries often assisted, with Italy being outstanding, and on occasion the support of Belgium or France has been considerable.

It is often argued that the pressures exerted on apartheid are futile, and simply harden the position. But the facts demonstrate the reverse. While South African sports administration, often dictated to by the politicians, have declared their determination never to change and never to abandon their policy, they have in fact made considerable modifications in an attempt to avoid total isolation in international sport. The most numerous were offered at Teheran, in an effort to avoid exclusion from Mexico. These included the agreement that, for the first time, there would be non-Whites in the party who would be permitted to wear a South African uniform and march under the South African flag and who would be allowed to travel together. This was being offered for the first time in history. In tennis and golf there have also been concessions. It would appear that non-Whites from other countries (but *not* from South Africa) will be permitted to take part in international team events in future. (The refusal of a visa to Arthur Ashe, the Black U.S. tennis champion, was based on two grounds: he was coming as an *individual* to take part in the championships and not as a member of a Davis Cup team, and secondly he was accused of having made political statements against apartheid.) But the biggest concession made thus far – since it touches rugby, the national game – is the one referred to earlier, namely, the total reversal by Mr. Vorster of the policy of Dr. Verwoerd, which excluded Maoris from the visiting All-Blacks (the name of the representative New Zealand rugby team – they had in fact always been all-White). Thus the team which toured South Africa in 1970 included two Maoris and one Samoan – admittedly they were very fair – and an Afrikaans paper, arguing for the inclusion of Maoris had pleaded that their skins were tea-coloured! But this was a major advance, and its consequences are as yet incalculable.

The tour evoked some interesting responses. It is fairly evident that non-Whites deliberately attended these matches to support the All-Blacks, and that they singled out the non-Whites in the side for special adulation – to the extreme irritation of White South Africa, and as a result non-Whites suffered ill-treatment at the hands of the police and of White spectators. Many non-Whites gloried in the successes of the All-Blacks and the discomfiture of the Whites; and some have gone on to ask the awkward question, why, if it is permissable for White South Africans to play against non-Whites from elsewhere, should it not be permissable for them to play against non-Whites of their own country?

A more interesting response has been that of the White South Africans who follow sports other than rugby, particularly the cricketers. They have seen their own tour of

Britain cancelled as a result of massive protest in Britain in retaliation of their Government's refusal to allow a non-White on the British team to South Africa. ("The D'Oliviera affair": the M.C.C. cancelled their tour of South Africa after being told that they could not select a non-White who had come from South Africa.) For them the question was, why should the rules of apartheid be bent for the sake of the rugby fans, but not in the case of other sports, many of whom were already forced into isolation?

It is this pressure which holds some interesting implications for the future.

Linked with it is another, whose future is less predictable. Emboldened by the mounting international pressures on racism in sport, and encouraged by the concessions given and the anguished cries of White sports administrators at the threat of increasing isolation, the leaders of the non-racial sports bodies have begun to make their own fresh thrust for international recognition and the removal of apartheid from sport. It is easier for them to do so, in a climate of White protest. As the *Guardian* pointed out in London, there was more protest from White sportsmen in South Africa against racism in sport in the ten days after the cancellation of the cricket tour than there had been in the preceding twenty years. However it is uncertain how long this protest will continue. But what is appearing in the country at the moment is the same kind of pressures which gave birth to S.A.S.A. and SAN-ROC and which promises similar successes.

Thus in September 1970 eight national non-racial sporting bodies met in conference and appealed to the White bodies to co-operate with them in seeking full international recognition for all sportsmen in the country, and warned that if the co-operation was not forthcoming, they would "go it alone".

There remains the final question. Where does all this protest in sport lead to? Can it really contribute to a total change of the apartheid society? The answer, oddly, must be yes, because South Africa is the odd kind of country it is – a country in which sport is an integral element in the fabric of the entire society.

Of course it might fail, but it will not be for lack of reasonableness. One need only look at the words of one of the spokesmen at the above mentioned sports conference – words that anywhere else would seem innocuous and even platitudinous, but which in South Africa have profound implications for the society: "It is not too much to ask of sportsmen of all races who love both sport and South Africa to speak out and make a call for the abolition of apartheid in all sport so that it can create, both within our borders and outside, interracial amity and good will."

Bibliography

Race and Sport, R. Thompson, Oxford University Press.
Seeds of Disaster, J. Laurence, Gollancz.
Racism and Sport, C. de Broglio, A Christian Aid pamphlet.
Sport and Race, M. Draper, South African Institute of Race Relations.
South Africa and the Olympics, M. Horrell, South African Institute of Race Relations.
The Bitter Choice, C. Legum, World Publications.

JAMES PITSE: African National Congress militant, somewhere in Africa. His poetry has been published in *Poems for Our Revolution*.

NO MAN SHALL SEE MY GRAVE

When the wind blows hot
And the stars are darkened
No man shall see my grave
With wreaths in South Africa.

No man shall see my grave
In the cemeteries of sorrow
If the compass of my ship fails **me**
For that ship will not be mine.

When waves become mountains
And skies are dark and mountainous
This ship of mine cannot sink
My people cannot sink.

No man shall see my grave
Before the evil sinks
Because death cannot bring life.
Death sometimes is desertion.

11 La Guma, Apartheid

The rivers of ice and sand
Cannot break my courage
The mountain of bombs and apartheid
Cannot stop my people.

They rule not my fate
They rule not my soul
They cannot bury me
Vultures cannot bury me.

No man shall see my grave
Where vultures fly
Where rivers flow with blood
And the fate of man is balanced.

My son shall see my grave
In waters clean and meadows cleansed
By our ship of freedom
A ship that cannot sink.

VINCENT GOABAKWE MATTHEWS (Joe): Attorney, educated at Fort Hare University College, Cape, before graduating in law. He was accused in the Treason Trial, 1956; and was a member of the African National Congress. Mr. Matthews worked in Botswana on the staff of the President's office for some years. An interview with the Johannesburg *Sunday Times* in April 1976 indicated that Mr. Matthews no longer holds the views he expresses here.

THE DEVELOPMENT OF THE
SOUTH AFRICAN REVOLUTION

Confronted by the inevitable difficulties of a complex struggle such as ours some people have become infected by false theories concerning our revolution. We are on the threshold of a great advance in our struggle for freedom based on mobilisation of the masses at home. The movement has scored some notable successes in the last few years. We have also sustained severe setbacks. A careful balance sheet will show that since Rivonia we have made a steady recovery of our initiative. But some people unable to see events in their totality pick on certain negative features and draw wildly generalised conclusions about the progress of our revolutionary struggle.

In the early part of this decade the A.N.C. and the liberation movement in general had to combat the idea that the struggle in South Africa would be a short one. In those days slogans promising freedom by a particular year were shouted by some irresponsible elements. The A.N.C. pointed out then that the struggle in South Africa would not follow the path by which many African countries achieved independence. We made it clear that negotiations and constitutional advance would not bring about our freedom. We said then that the struggle would be long and difficult. History has proved that those who thought the struggle would be brief were utterly wrong.

As is usual with petite bourgeoisie intellectuals the same elements have now swung to the other extreme. Confronted by a tough and long revolutionary struggle the people who were prattling about a quick victory have become the biggest pessimists. Basing themselves on the great disparity in military strength and resources between ourselves and the enemy they conclude that there is little hope of a change in the situation. This attitude also is quite wrong. The situation in our country is not static but rapidly developing in many different directions. The period of lull is rapidly coming to a close. The reactionary offensive that has marked the last nine years has now lost impetus.

Faced with a growing armed revolution in Southern Africa the ruling classes in our country are beginning to commit strategic mistakes with far-reaching consequences for the future. Recent divisions within the ruling group reflected differences in the strategy for preserving White supremacy. The contradictions that have always been inherent in the South African social structure are growing acute. Provided the movement gives clear leadership and puts forward correct strategic and tactical plans and directives as well as selfless organisational work, an upturn in the struggle is inevitable.

Our movement must be orientated on the perspective of a struggle that will be fairly protracted but will undoubtedly be crowned with success.

The armed revolution in Algeria took about eight years before victory was achieved. In heroic Vietnam the struggle has been going on for decades first against the French and then against the United States. The revolution in Angola began eight years ago and has registered big successes. The struggle in Guinea (Bissau) and in Mozambique have similarly gone on for some time now.

Like all oppressed peoples we would naturally like to get rid of the oppressors and exploiters in the shortest possible time. Should it turn out that the revolution develops faster than expected we should be ready for that. But any serious analysis seems to suggest that our struggle will be a long one.

The ruling oligarchy in our country has been entrenched in power for a long period. Everything has been done to deprive the majority of the people of any element of power. The coercive machinery of the state is virtually entirely manned by the members of the privileged White minority. The enemy has at his disposal all the resources of a wealthy and fairly developed modern state. Last but no means least the enemy has been able to count on the many-sided support of the major imperialist powers.

On the other hand the oppressed people start off the armed struggle with a number of serious disadvantages. The most important of them is relative absence of military equipment and techniques. The people also have not acquired knowledge of the method of guerrilla warfare in the mass. To correct these weaknesses will be a slow process during the course of developing our armed revolutionary struggle. Why then in spite of the factors mentioned above are we so absolutely certain of victory?

The fundamental and decisive factor to bear in mind

is that the national liberation movement is historically and socially a progressive force fighting for a better life for the people. The enemy on the other hand fights under the banner of reaction to protect ill-gotten gains and privileges enjoyed by the minority at the expense of the people. The policy of imperialist and colonialist suppression of the people is retrogressive and doomed to defeat. On no account can the enemy ever gain support from the people for a policy of suppressing them. This is a fundamental and permanent feature of the situation which is often undervalued, precisely because it is so obvious. But in a prolonged armed revolution it is the factor that more and more determines the side which wins.

Very powerful social forces stand fundamentally opposed to the present regime. The national movement of the oppressed Africans, Indians and Coloured people stand opposed to the regime. The forces of social change among the workers, peasants, and intellectuals stand opposed to the regime. These forces have within them tremendous power when organised. The onset of every new form of struggle has the immediate tendency to temporarily disrupt organisation. This happened in our case also at different times in our history. When the period of non-violent struggle came to an end it found the liberation movement in our country in possession of a stable leadership in command of a relatively well organised mass movement. The adoption of the decision to wage armed struggle for the overthrow of the regime involved a complete change of strategy, tactics, propaganda, organisational machinery and so on. This could not but result in some disruption of organisation to say nothing of the fact that the reaction of the enemy added further difficulties.

The Morogoro conference had laid the basis both in principle and in organisation for a complete remoulding of our movement so as to enable full utilisation of our those forces opposed to the continued existence of the that in conditions such as obtain in our police-ridden country it is not possible to organise the masses except as part of and in conjunction with the waging of armed struggle.

It is also necessary to get rid of the concept that the masses will be organised by a few people at the top. Our experience teaches that the masses of the people display great organisational initiative themselves. We must make it possible for our numerous activists and supporters to do organisational work in support of the armed struggle. Whilst we begin the struggle in a relatively weak position in so far as military technique and arm supplies are concerned, this is not permanent. Step by step, our people must acquire both the techniques of war and the means for fighting such a war.

In the resistance war it is not practical to achieve complete co-ordination and unity of the national liberation and progressive forces under the leadership of the A.N.C. This means that an authoritative organ for prosecuting the revolution is now being built with the full support of all those forces opposed to the continued existence of the present fascist regime. No organisation outside the United Front built around the A.N.C. and its allies exists which is capable of leading the struggle. All reformists and opportunist groupings which at one time existed in our country have disintegrated both ideologically and organisationally. This is an extremely favourable factor for conducting the revolutionary war.

We have said that the resources of the South African regime are great relative to ours at the moment. But this must not be exaggerated. South Africa is not a world power and the privileged minority is numerically small. In the long run this weakness of the enemy will tell very much.

A vital factor making for our inevitable victory is that our struggle has the support of friends all over the world. Firstly we have direct allies in the millions who support the armed struggle in our neighbouring countries of Namibia, Angola, Zimbabwe, Mozambique. In particular the alliance with ZAPU (Zimbabwe African Peoples' Union) and the people of Zimbabwe is of great importance to our prospects of victory.

As the struggle develops in our country it will reach a level which will oblige neighbouring countries to increase their support to our people. At the moment some of our neighbours who sympathise with our case are hesitating and wavering under the threats of the fascists. A time will come when the level of the struggle in South Africa will enable our neighbours to come out in their true colours of genuine supporters of the oppressed people in our country. At that stage any government that did not support the armed struggle of our people would be overthrown by the masses in the neighbouring countries who know full well the evils of apartheid and fascism.

In other African countries we have to take the long view. Some countries like Malawi are taking a direction hostile to our struggle and collaborating with our enemies. Others take up political and economic positions of which we, as the representatives of the South African people, disapprove. It will not be possible for these countries to take up positions which we in the A.N.C. dislike, the moment the struggle in our country reaches what might be called the "critical point". Our immediate task is to work hard to achieve the requisite level of armed struggle in our country. But there is no doubt that in the long run the independent African states will form a major part of support for our struggle.

Further afield are the Afro-Asian states, the Latin American countries, the Socialist states which already play a vital role in isolating apartheid and its allies internationally. This international support will eventually be translated into massive direct resistance to our armed struggle. Hence it is important constantly to develop our international work as an aid not only now but in the future.

To sum up then, our struggle for liberation is likely to

be a prolonged one and we must base our actions and planning with that as our orientation. This does not mean we have all the time in the world. It is necessary to work hard and selflessly to achieve the overthrow of the disastrous apartheid regime as fast as possible. But we consider that the struggle will be long and we must get our people and our friends and supporters to understand the implications of this perspective.

On the other hand our victory is absolutely certain. Both historically and in practical terms the conditions now exist which were not there ten years ago for a successful revolutionary war in our country.

The basic character of the regime in our country has not changed. The fascist regime has now been in power in South Africa for twenty-one years. This has caused some people to compare the longevity of the regime with those of Spain and Portugal. There are important differences. For one thing the Spanish and Portuguese fascist regimes are ruling respectively Spaniards and Portuguese. In South Africa the small White privileged minority has imposed fascism on what is really a huge colonially oppressed people. Such a regime can no longer be tolerated in a resurgent Africa. The empires of Spain and Portugal in Africa are similarly headed for collapse.

During this whole period of fascist rule the reactionary offensive and terror directed against the people have steadily grown. The arsenal of fiendish laws becomes larger. Reprisals and torture of freedom fighters claim a growing list of victims. Thousands of the finest people in our country are imprisoned in the gaols of the oppressors. The notorious pass laws are ever more stringently applied. Military preparations have reached a level at which they now play a significant role in the economy.

The grim picture of national oppression and exploitation is in no way modified by the so-called "Homelands" policy or by the much vaunted economic "boom" about which we hear so much. South Africa is a fascist state with no redeeming features. Such a regime must be overthrown and all efforts must be concentrated on just that.

The talk of an economic boom has arisen from the swift development that has taken place in the industrial sector of the economy. It should be stressed that the chief motive force of this development has been precisely low wages, tough labour laws, absence of social security, no trade unions, no political rights, exploitation of the vast majority of the people, especially the African people. To turn round and ask the oppressed people to congratulate the regime for an economic progress brought about through their misery and from which they do not benefit is the sheerest gall and impudence on the part of the regime and its servitors.

An economy based on this primitive exploitation of the bulk of the people coupled with a ruthless policy designed to deprive them of skills contains a fundamental weakness. Further progress and economic growth require an end to the colour bars in industry, education and politics. Apartheid has now become a major barrier to the growth of the economy and to its integration with its natural hinterland in the rest of the African continent.

The general tendency is to compare the economic position of South Africa with that of other African states and this makes it appear as if the economy is strong. In fact by international standards South Africa is a backward country. Of course, to the apologists of the regime, "South Africa" means the White people, who enjoy a high standard of living at the expense of the non-White people. But if one has regard to the economic indices that distinguish backward from advanced countries it will be seen that South Africa is way behind. In terms of *per capita* income; health services; education; housing; transport; cultural and recreational facilities, the country is backward.

The overthrow of apartheid has now become an essential element in any policy of continued economic growth and progress of the country.

One positive factor in the economic developments of the last few years has been the tempestuous growth of the working class. Economic laws are operating to expand the working class and especially the industrial working class. Sooner or later this mighty force will make itself felt and rock the regime to its foundations.

The armed struggle cannot be developed without a clear attitude to the land question which affects the bulk of the South African oppressed people. The people in the Reserves, on European farms and on the huge plantations must know that in fighting they are aiming at the seizing of the land from those who illegally and unjustifiably control it today. What economic policies will be followed in liberated areas will depend on the concrete conditions obtaining them, and on the need to sustain the struggle and develop it further. In the initial period we must expect the position to be untidy and according to armchair revolutionaries, even chaotic. But there is no possibility of developing guerrilla struggle without making it very clear that the liberation movement is calling on the people to fight for the land and to drive off the farms and plantations all those who have ruthlessly exploited the people. The land barons must be driven off the land which must be taken over by those who actually work it.

The revolutionary potential of the rural masses is very great. It is only under conditions of armed struggle that it becomes possible to organise those on the European farms. The urban proletariat is destined to be the vanguard of the struggle in our country not only by reason of its advanced social and organisational role but also because of its numerical strength. The revolution in our country cannot succeed unless the working class is mobilised and exercises hegemony over the revolution in practice and in fact. No other class exists in our country that can exercise the role of leader and organiser of the revolution. The middle class and petite bourgeoisie elements among the oppressed people are too weak to play the role of vanguard. So that in our country the vanguard role of the working class is not only a matter of preference, it is an actual necessity as it is the only class that can exercise hegemony in the revolution and in its consolidation after the victory of the revolution. This truth about our country ought to be grasped firmly and put into practice in our policies. We have to admit that the consequences of this have not yet been fully grasped by all sectors of the national movement although there is a general, unguided and almost unconscious movement in that direction.

Our struggle would make much faster progress if the theoretical and practical implications of working-class leadership of our national movement were understood. Often this issue is unjustifiably confused with another. Our movement is organised under the banner of the African National Congress which leads the national democratic revolution. The liberation of the African people is the main content of the democratic revolution. But in order to succeed and in order that the revolution should be carried through to the end it is essential that the working class of our country which has and continues to bear the brunt of the struggle must have hegemony of the whole liberation movement. What this means and how it is organisationally reflected requires the attention of all sectors of the movement.

There is no possibility of securing changes in our country except through revolution. Faced with temporary difficulties, some people, especially outside our own movement, are beginning to toy with all manner of reformist theories. These find currency in the realm of Bantustan politics. Some intellectuals have decided to participate in politics as supporters of "separate development". In the Transkei and elsewhere some people, for selfish reasons, are endeavouring to justify government policy. The Bantustans have now been established in the Northern Transvaal, Western Transvaal, Ciskei and Transkei. We have just had elections for the Coloured Representative Council. The Indian Council has also been set up. Does all this suggest that we are now in a period of retreat in which reform comes to the fore as a tactic?

The reformist experiments are a cruel farce. The whole of Africa is virtually free from foreign rule. Independent states have sprung up on the borders of and within the Republic of South Africa. In the still colonial territories the people are waging heroic guerrilla struggles for their freedom. South Africa is no exception to the developments taking place in the rest of Africa.

Reformism in our country historically failed in a very long period to lead our people to freedom. On the contrary the most sustained reformist policies led to the fascism and terror we experience today. There is not one single fact to justify any expectation that reform could even lead to any amelioration of our conditions. Our history and experience have taught us very harsh lessons. One of the most vital is that without building an army, arming our people and conducting revolutionary struggle we will remain an oppressed and exploited people. The only correct path for the oppressed national groups and their democratic supporters among the Whites is armed revolutionary struggle. This is not altered by the problems and difficulties that confront us in developing the revolution.

Our movement has the experience and resources to make the changes and efforts needed to carry out our revolution. The decisions of Morogoro lay the basis for utilising all the talents of our people for the tasks that lie ahead. New elements need to be brought into leading positions at every level in order to reinforce and provide necessary renewal of our movement. It is necessary to enable all our people to be mobilised for the revolutionary struggle. Up to now we have not done nearly enough positive mobilisation of the masses of our people. They have been mobilised in a negative sort of way by the enemy. The enemy press and radio have been very busy telling the people about the guerrilla struggles in Zimbabwe, Mozambique and Angola. They have conducted vicious propaganda campaigns against our movement and its leaders. They have sent information officers all over the rural areas telling the people to "co-operate" with the government in crushing the guerrilla movement. This is telling the people about the revolution and making them curious about it. But this is a negative mobilisation conducted by our enemies against our interests.

We have to see that the voice of the movement itself reaches the masses by all means possible. The people have to be drawn into the manifold tasks of the revolution. Our theory of revolution must become the possession of all our people.

The African National Congress has undertaken the responsibility of organising not only the African people but all national groups in the struggle for the overthrow of the fascist regime. This means that organisational forms have to be built by the A.N.C. for this purpose. This will facilitate not only the revolutionary struggle but will project the A.N.C. as the alternative to the present regime of White supremacy. We do not just want change. Our national liberation movement desires to remake society in a new and just way. Our programme, the Freedom Charter, offers the way out of the present crisis brought about by apartheid.

A big campaign must be waged at all levels of our movement to bring about understanding of our policies, strategy and tactics. On the basis of a profound understanding it is possible to build a strong, united and disciplined movement with a leadership that enjoys the unqualified support and confidence of the people. This cannot be achieved by administrative means but only on the basis of people who consciously understand what they are fighting for and how they will achieve victory.

Our people have great experience of politics and have participated consistently in struggle for many decades.

They have built organisations in which they have confidence. Thousands of our colleagues who languish in the gaols of the enemy place their hopes on the movement. Whilst it is true that we need a big expansion of propaganda and ideological work, basically the people of South Africa are looking for a movement that can provide practical and effective methods of struggle against the apartheid regime. We are convinced that faithful application of the decisions of the Morogoro conference will lead to the successful beginning and prosecution of armed revolution in our country.

BARRY FEINBERG: Artist and poet. Born 1938, in Germiston, South Africa; studied at Johannesburg School of Art and at The Slade, London. He left South Africa in 1960 and now works for the literary executors of Bertrand Russell, London. Mr. Feinberg has compiled and edited *The Archives of Bertrand Russell*, 1967, and *Dear Bertrand Russell* (letters), 1969. He has had several exhibitions of paintings in London and his poems have been published in various anthologies.

TEN TARGETS REEL UNDER RAGE OF VISION

After years of bruising loads
heaved picks and burning girders,
knotted limbs and bitter knuckles cracking,
a gun lies lightly on the shoulder.
A big gun of many assemblies,
smooth bullets coil toothing at the neck,
grenades hung from hip gently swinging.

Once a volunteer under Gandhi colours,
head bleeding from double bludgeon
for turning cheek to set right thinking.
Then haunted by post-midnight squads,
splintered doors, splattered walls,
kicks and children clinging.
Months of guards beating in bleak yards,
conscience brothers thinned and shaking
some, green veined through static charges
another crazy dangled by borrowed belt.

This felt a thousand times repeated:
sons long left to memories yearning
a face loved, fades while reappearing,
home, a mirage of vapoured living.

Now,
memories feed round embered flame,
an Impala, fresh impaled, fat sizzles
burning carbon crust to stave a day's march.

Tomorrow,
maybe no game but combat coming.

Then,
that fast drop to knee
fierce burst of fire,
quick dodge and crawl
and back track to cover.

This,
a fine tuned, harsh handled man
hard as nails and head well guided;
no computer type reaction
no lathe like operation,
but thought out, mind planned,
hands trim on hair-taut trigger.
His eyes blaze down dead-still barrel,
ten targets reel under rage of vision.

A Political Report adopted by the Consultative Conference of the A.N.C. at the Morogoro Conference, Tanzania, May 1969.

STRATEGY AND TACTICS OF THE SOUTH AFRICAN REVOLUTION

The struggle of the oppressed people of South Africa is taking place within an international context of transition to the Socialist system, of the breakdown of the colonial system as a result of national liberation and socialist revolutions, and the fight for social and economic progress by the people of the whole world.

We in South Africa are part of the zone in which national liberation is the chief content of the struggle. On our continent sweeping advances have been registered which have resulted in the emergence to independent statehood of forty-one states. Thus the first formal step of independence has been largely won in Africa and this fact exercises a big influence on the developments in our country.

The countries of Southern Africa have not as yet broken the chains of colonialism and racism which hold them in oppression. In Mozambique, Angola, South West Africa, Zimbabwe and South Africa White racialist and fascist regimes maintain systems which go against the current trend of the African revolution and world development.

This has been made possible by the tremendous economic and military power at the disposal of these regimes built with the help of imperialism.

The main pillar of the unholy alliance of Portugal, Rhodesia and South Africa is the Republic of South Africa. The strategy and tactics of our revolution require for their formulation and understanding a full appreciation of the interlocking and interweaving of international, African and Southern African developments which play on our situation.

South Africa was conquered by force and is today ruled by force. At moments when White autocracy feels itself threatened, it does not hesitate to use the gun. When the gun is not in use, legal and administrative terror, fear, social and economic pressures, complacency and confusion generated by propaganda and "education", are the devices brought into play in an attempt to harness the people's opposition. Behind these devices hovers force. Whether in reserve or in actual employment, force is ever present and this has been so since the White man came to Africa.

From the time alien rule was imposed there has been, historically, unbroken resistance to this domination. It has taken different forms at different times but it has never been abandoned. For the first 250 years there were regular armed clashes, battles and wars. The superior material resources of the enemy, the divided and often fragmented nature of the resistance, the unchallenged ascendancy of imperialism, as a world system up to the beginning of the twentieth century, the historically under-standable absence of political cohesion and leadership in the people's camp; these and other factors combined to end the first phase of resistance unequalled anywhere else in Africa are underlined by the fact that the armed sub-jugation of the indigenous people was only really accom-plished at the beginning of this century.

The defeat of the Bambata Rebellion in 1906 marked the end of this first phase and set the stage for the hand-ing over of the administration of the country to local Whites in 1910. The fifty years which followed was not a period of resignation or of acceptance. It was a period of development and of regrouping under new conditions; a period in which newly created political formations of the people continued to struggle with the enemy and grew into maturity; a period in which, above all, national conscious-ness began to assert itself against tribal sectionalism. This period witnessed the emergence and development of the primary organisation of the liberation movement – the African National Congress. It also saw the evolvement of national organisations reflecting the aspirations of other oppressed non-White groups – the Coloureds and In-dians – and the creation of economic and political organi-sations – the South African Communist Party, Trade Unions which reflected the special aims and aspirations of the newly developed and doubly exploited working class. This was a period of organisational growth. It was punc-tuated by struggles involving techniques ranging from orthodox mass campaigning to general strikes, to mass acts of defiance. It culminated in the decision taken in 1961 to prepare for armed confrontation. The year 1961 saw the opening stages of this campaign in the simultaneous acts of sabotage which occurred in most of the main urban centres on 16 December.

Why was the decision for armed struggle taken in 1961? Why not 1951 or 1941 or 1931? Is it that the character of the state has so altered fundamentally that only in 1961 did armed struggle become the only alternative? Not at all. There has never been a moment in the history of South Africa since 1652 in which the White ruling class would have given privileges without a physical battle. Why then did organisations like the African National Congress not call for armed struggle? Was it perhaps that they were not really revolutionary or that it was only in the early 'sixties that they began to appreciate the correct strategy? Is there perhaps substance in the accusations by some of our detractors that until the early 'sixties the liberation movement was lacking in military fervour and the desire for radical change? In other words was its policy not a revolutionary one? What is our measuring rod for revolutionary policy? A look at this concept will help towards a more profound understanding not only of the past but of the future. It is therefore not out of place to devote a word to it.

In essence, a revolutionary policy is one which holds out the quickest and most fundamental transformation and transfer of power from one class to another. In real life such radical changes are brought about not by imaginary forces but by those whose outlook and readiness to act is very much influenced by historically determined factors.

To ignore the real situation and to play about with imaginary forces, concepts and ideals is to invite failure. The art of revolutionary leadership consists in providing leadership to the masses and not just to its most advanced elements; it consists of setting a pace which accords with objective conditions and the real possibilities at hand. The revolutionary sounding phrase does not always reflect revolutionary policy, and revolutionary sounding policy is not always the springboard for revolutionary advance.

Indeed, what appears to be "militant" and "revolutionary" can often be counter-revolutionary. It is surely a question of whether, in the given concrete situation, the course or policy advocated will aid or impede the prospects of the conquest of power. In this – the only test – the advocacy of armed struggle can, in some situations, be as counter-revolutionary as the advocacy of its opposite in other situations. Untimely, ill-planned or premature manifestations of violence impede and do not advance the prospect for revolutionary change and are clearly counter-revolutionary. It is obvious therefore that policy and organisational structures must grow out of the real situation if they are not to become meaningless clichés.

Future historians may well be able to pause at some moments during the evolution of our struggle and examine critically both its pace and emphasis. But, in general, without the so-called reformist activities of the previous half century, the prospect of advancing into the new phase would have been extremely small. This is so because even in the typical colonial-type situation armed struggle becomes feasible only if:

There is disillusionment with the prospect of achieving liberation by traditional peaceful processes because the objective conditions blatantly bar the way to change;
There is readiness to respond to the strategy of armed struggle with all the enormous sacrifices which this involves;
There is in existence a political leadership capable of gaining the organised allegiance of the people for armed struggle and which has both the experience and the ability to carry out the painstaking process of planning, preparation and overall conduct of the operations;
There exist favourable objective conditions in the international and local plans.

In one sense conditions are connected and interdependent. They are not created by subjective and ideological activity only and many are the mistakes committed by heroic revolutionaries who give a monopoly to the subjective factor and who confuse their own readiness with the readiness of others.

These conditions are brought about not only by developing political, economic and social conditions but also by the long, hard grind of revolutionary work. They depend on such factors as the response of the enemy, the extent to which he unmasks himself and the experience gained by the people themselves not in academic seminars but in actual political struggle.

We reject the approach which sees as the catalyst for revolutionary transformation only the short cut of isolated confrontations and the creation of armed resistance centres. Does this mean that before an actual beginning can be made to the armed challenge we have to wait for the evolvement of some sort of deep crisis in the enemy camp which is serious enough to hold out the possibility of an immediate all-round insurrection? Certainly not! We believe that given certain basic factors, both international and local, the actual beginning of armed struggle or guerrilla warfare can be made and having begun can steadily develop conditions for the future all-out war which will eventually lead to the conquest of power. Under the modern highly sophisticated police state (which South Africa is) it is questionable whether a movement can succeed in a programme of mass political organisation beyond a certain point without starting a new type of action. Also, it is not easy to determine the point at which sufficient concrete political and organisational preparations have been carried out to give our armed detachments the maximum chances of survival and growth within any given area. There is no instrument for measuring this. But we must not overdo the importance of the subjective factor and before embarking upon a path which is in one sense tragic, although historically inevitable and necessary, certain of the basic minimum conditions already mentioned must be present and certain minimum preparations must have been made.

In the light of those considerations, it is clear that it was only after the victory of the anti-imperialist forces in the Second World War and the tide of independence in

Africa, Asia and Latin America, combined with the zig-zags of struggle inside South Africa in the last fifty years which by the beginning of the 'sixties demanded a move in the direction of armed struggle. The 'fifties were among the most stirring and struggle-filled decades in the history of the liberation movement. Thousands upon thousands of militant cadres were tempered during this period and masses of our people both in town and countryside participated in a variety of forms of struggle. The moulding of mass political consciousness reached a new intensity. The response of the authorities was such that the overwhelming majority of the people learnt, through their own participation in the struggle and confrontation with the state, that in the long run the privileges of the minority will only be wrenched from it by a reversion to armed combat. Indeed, during this "peaceful" stage in our struggle hardly a year passed without massacres of our people by the army and police.

Each phase in the unfolding of the struggle of the 'fifties played a part in setting the stage of our new approach. A rebirth of the spirit of deliberate defiance of the White man's law was stimulated by the great Defiance Campaign of 1952. The response of the state towards the Congress of the People Campaign and the adoption of the Freedom Charter demonstrated its intention to crush what had previously been accepted as legitimate expressions for equality. The numbers of highly successful national general strikes motivated in the main by political and not economic demands proved the growing maturity of the urban non-White working class. The magnificent resistance by the peasants in Pondoland, Sekhukhuniland and Natal in the late 'fifties pointed also to the new spirit of militancy and struggle in the countryside.

The general strike as a method of political mobilisation was suppressed with the utmost vigour and by the end of the 'fifties could no longer be effectively employed as an instrument of mass struggle. Other protests were increasingly broken by police brutality and the use of orthodox mass demonstration as an effective weapon was demonstrably no longer feasible. Legal opposition was rendered ineffective by bannings, exiles and the imprisonment of activists and leaders to long terms for the most trivial infringements. Finally by such laws as the Terrorism and Sabotage Acts all opposition by the legal or peaceful means was rendered impossible.

In the field of representation, any reformist illusion that may still have existed of a slow advance towards democracy was shattered by the removal of the historic remains of non-White representation including even undemocratic and powerless bodies such as the Native Representative Council. Thus the enemy unmasked himself completely not only to a group of advanced thinkers but to the mass of the people as a whole. The liberation surge towards independence of the African continent which marked the late 'fifties and early 'sixties had an important bearing on our own situation. Not only were friendly borders creeping closer but in a very real way these events stimulated and excited people in the unliberated territories in the direction of self-rule. The basic drive for this in our country had never been suppressed. But the events in South Africa in the previous decade and what was happening on the continent confirmed that conquest of power by the people was a realisable goal in our lifetime. The enormous material power of the enemy and by contrast the material weakness of the people was to them no more than a temporary impediment. The memory of Cuba and – on our continent – of Algeria, was fresh, both had proved that in the long run material resources alone are not a determining factor.

The heightened political ferment both here and on our continent reflected itself in the growth and further maturing of all sections of the liberation front. Those leaders who were unable to adjust to the new revolutionary mood (even before the policy of the preparations for organised armed resistance) fell by the wayside. The cohesion and unity of action between the various national and social groupings comprising the liberation front reached new heights. All this constituted not only moral justification for a move towards armed struggle, but, what is more important, conditions had been created – they were not always there – making a departure in this direction correct, necessary and, in the true sense, revolutionary.

In a way the decision taken in 1961 was, historically speaking, in the tradition of the earlier armed resistance to the entrenchment of the foreigner. But it is now occurring in a new situation. Not only had this situation to be understood but the art and science – both politically and military – of armed liberation struggles in the modern epoch had to be grasped and applied. The head-on mobile warfare of the traditional African armies of the past could not meet the challenge. The riot, the street fight, the outbursts of unorganised violence, individual terrorism; these were symptoms of the militant spirit but not pointers to revolutionary technique. The winning of our freedom by armed struggle – the only method left open to us – demands more than passion. It demands an understanding and an implementation of revolutionary theory and techniques in the actual conditions facing us. It demands a sober assessment of the obstacles in our way and an appreciation that such a struggle is bitter and protracted. It demands too the dominance in our thinking of achievement over drama. We believe our movement acted in accordance with these guidelines when it embarked upon the detailed preparation for the launching of guerrilla struggle.

We understood that the main physical environment of such a struggle in the initial period is outside the enemy strongholds in the cities, in the vast stretches of our countryside. The opening steps in 1961 – organised sabotage mainly in the urban areas – served a special purpose and was never advanced as a technique which would, on its

187

own, either lead to the destruction of the state or even do it great material damage (although guerrilla activity in the urban areas of a special type is always important as an auxiliary). At the same time there was a threefold need to be met in order to lay the foundations for more developed and meaningful armed activity of the guerrilla type.

The first was the need to create a military apparatus and, more particularly to recruit large numbers of professional cadres who were to be trained and who would form the core of future guerrilla bands.

The second was the need to demonstrate effectively that we were making a sharp and open break with the processes of the previous period which had correctly given emphasis to militant struggle short of armed confrontation.

The third was the need to present an effective method for the overthrow of White supremacy through planned rather than spontaneous activity. The sabotage campaign was an earnest indication of our seriousness in the pursuit of this new strategy. All three needs were served by this convincing evidence that our liberation movement had correctly adjusted itself to the new situation and was creating an apparatus actually capable of clandestinely hitting the enemy and making preparation for a more advanced phase. The situation was such that without activity of this nature our whole political leadership may have been at stake both inside and outside the country and the steps which were simultaneously taken for the recruitment and preparation of military cadres would have met with less response.

When we talk of revolutionary armed struggle, we are talking of political struggle by means which include the use of military force even though once force as a tactic is introduced it has the most far-reaching consequences on every aspect of our activities. It is important to emphasise this because our movement must reject all manifestations of militarism which separates armed people's struggle from its political context.

Reference has already been made to the danger of the thesis which regards the creation of military areas as the generator of mass resistance. But even more is involved in this concept. One of the vital problems connected with this bears on the important question of the relationship between the political and military. From the very beginning our movement has brooked no ambiguity concerning this. The primacy of the political leadership is unchallenged and supreme and all revolutionary formations and levels (whether armed or not) are subordinate to this leadership. To say this is not just to invoke tradition. This approach is rooted in the very nature of this type of revolutionary struggle and is borne out by the experience of the overwhelming majority of revolutionary movements which have engaged in such struggles. Except in very rare instances, the people's armed challenge against a foe with formidable material strength does not achieve dramatic and swift success. The path is filled with obstacles and we harbour no illusions on this score in the case of South Africa. In the long run it can only succeed if it attracts the active support of the mass of the people. Without this lifeblood it is doomed. Even in our country with the historical background and traditions of armed resistance still within the memory of many people and the special developments of the immediate past, the involvement of the masses is unlikely to be the result of a sudden, natural and automatic consequence of military clashes.

It has to be won in all-round political mobilisation which must accompany the military activities. This includes educational and agitational work throughout the country to cope with the sophisticated torrent of misleading propaganda and "information" of the enemy which will become more intense as the struggle sharpens. When armed clashes begin they seldom involve more than a comparative handful of combatants whose very conditions of fighting existence make them incapable of exercising the functions of all-round political leadership. The masses of the peasants, workers and youth, beleaguered for a long time by the enemy's military occupation, have to be activated in a multitude of ways not only to ensure a growing stream of recruits for the fighting units but to harass the enemy politically so that his forces are dispersed and therefore weakened. This calls for the exercise of all-round political leadership.

Guerrilla warfare, the special, and in our case the only form in which the armed liberation struggle can be launched, is neither static nor does it take place in a vacuum. The tempo, the overall strategy to be employed, the opening of new fronts, the progression from lower to higher forms, thence to mobile warfare; these and other vital questions cannot be solved by the military leadership alone, they require overall political judgments intimately involved with the people both inside and outside the actual areas of armed combat. If mere awareness of oppression combined with heroic examples by armed bands were enough, the struggle would indeed be simple. There would be no collaborators and it would be hard to find neutrals. But to believe this is to believe that the course of struggle is determined solely by what we do in the fighting units and further involves the fallacious assumption that the masses are rock-like and incorruptible. The enemy is as aware as we are that the side that wins the allegiance of the people wins the struggle. It is naive to believe that oppressed and beleaguered people cannot temporarily, even in large numbers, be won over by fears, terror, lies, indoctrination, and provocation to treat liberators as enemies. In fact history proves that without the most intensive all-round political activity this is the more likely result. It is therefore all the more vital that the revolutionary leadership is nation-wide and has its roots both inside and outside the actual areas of combat. Above all, when victory comes, it must not be a hollow one. To ensure this we must also ensure that what is brought to power is not an army but the masses as a whole at the head of which stands its organised political leadership. This is the perspective which is rooted at all levels of our liberation movement whether within or outside the army. Our confidence in final victory rests not on the wish or the dream but on our understanding of our own conditions and the historical processes. This understanding must be deepened and must spread to every level of our movement. We must have a clear grasp not only of ourselves and of our own forces but also of the enemy – of his power and vulnerability. Guerrilla struggle is certainly no exception to the rule that depth of understanding, and knowledge of realities, both favourable and unfavourable, make for more lasting commitment and more illuminating leadership. How then do we view the enemy we face – his strength and his weakness? What sort of structure do we face and how dogged will the enemy resistance be?

On the face of it the enemy is in stable command of a rich and varied economy which, even at this stage when it is not required to extend itself, can afford an enormous military budget. He has a relatively well trained and efficient army and police force. He can draw on fairly large man power resources. In addition the major imperialist powers such as Britain, West Germany, France, the United States and Japan who have an enormous stake in the economy of our country constitute a formidable support for the apartheid regime. Even now before the crisis deepens the imperialist partners of South Africa have done much to develop the economy and armament programme of South Africa. In a situation of crisis they may pass over from support to active intervention to save the racist regime.

If there is one lesson that the history of guerrilla struggle has taught it is that the material strength and resources of the enemy is by no means a decisive factor. Guerrilla warfare almost by definition presents a situation in which there is a vast imbalance of material and military resources between the opposing sides. It is designed to cope with the situation in which the enemy is infinitely superior in relation to every conventional factor of warfare. It is *par excellence* the weapon of the materially weak against the materially strong. Given its popular character and given a population which increasingly sides with and shields the guerrilla whilst at the same time opposing and exposing the enemy, the survival and growth of a people's army is assured by the skilful exercise of tactics. Surprise, mobility and tactical retreat should make it difficult for the enemy to bring into play its superior fire power in any decisive battles. No individual battle is fought in circumstances favourable to the enemy. Superior forces can thus be harassed, weakened and, in the end, destroyed. The absence of an orthodox front, of fighting lines; the need of the enemy to attenuate his resources and lines of communication over vast areas; the need to protect the widely scattered installations on which his economy is dependent; these are among the factors which serve in the long run to compensate in favour of the guerrilla for the disparity in the starting strength of the adversaries. The words "in the long run" must be stressed because it would be idle to dispute the considerable military advantages to the enemy of his high level industrialisation, his ready-to-hand reserves of White man power and his excellent roads, railways and air transport which facilitate swift manoeuvres and speedy concentration of personnel. But we must not overlook the fact that over a period of time many of these unfavourable factors will begin to operate in favour of the liberation forces:

> The ready-to-hand resources including food production depend overwhelmingly on non-White labour which, with the growing intensity of the struggle, will not remain docile and co-operative;
> The White man power resources may seem adequate initially but must become dangerously stretched as guerrilla warfare develops. Already extremely

short of skilled labour – the monopoly of the Whites – the mobilisation of a large force for a protracted struggle will place a further burden on the workings of the economy;

In contrast to many other major guerrilla struggles, the enemy's economic and man power resources are all situated within the theatre of war and there is no secure external pool (other than direct intervention by a foreign state) safe from sabotage, mass action and guerrilla action on which the enemy can draw;

The very sophistication of the economy with its well developed system of communications makes it a much more vulnerable target. In an undeveloped country the interruption of supplies to any given region may be no more than a local setback. In a highly sensitive modern structure of the South African type, the successful harassment of transport to any major industrial complex inevitably inflicts immense damage to the economy as a whole and to the morale of the enemy.

One of the more popular misconceptions concerning guerrilla warfare is that a physical environment which conforms to a special pattern is indispensible – thick jungle, inaccessible mountain areas, swamps, a friendly border and so on. The availability of this sort of terrain is, of course, of tremendous advantage to the guerrillas especially in the early non-operational phase when training and other preparatory steps are undertaken and no external bases are available for this purpose. When operations commence, the guerrilla cannot survive, let alone flourish, unless he moves to areas where people live and work and where the enemy can be engaged in combat. If he is fortunate enough to have behind him a friendly border or areas of difficult access which can provide temporary refuge it is, of course, advantageous. But guerrilla warfare can be, and has been, waged in every conceivable type of terrain, in deserts, swamps, in farm fields, in built-up areas, in plains, in the bush and in countries without friendly borders or islands surrounded by the sea. This whole question is one of adjusting survival tactics to the sort of terrain in which operations have to be carried out.

In any case, in the vast expanse that is South Africa, a people's force will find a multitude of variations in topography, deserts, mountains, forests, veld and swamps. There might not appear to be a single impregnable mountain or impenetrable jungle but the country abounds in terrain which in general is certainly no less favourable for guerrilla operations than some of the terrain in which other guerrilla movements operated successfully. Also the issue must be looked at in the context of guerrillas, who are armed and operate in the terrain. The combination makes an area impregnable for the guerrilla. South Africa's tremendous size will make it extremely difficult, if not impossible, for the White regime to keep the whole of it under armed surveillance in strength and in depth. Hence, an early development of a relatively safe (though shifting) rear is not beyond the realm of practicality.

The above are only some of the important factors which have not always been studied and understood. It is necessary to stress these factors not only because they give balance to our efforts but because – properly assessed – they help destroy the myth of the enemy's invincibility.

But above all a scientific revolutionary strategy demands a correct appreciation of the political character of the forces which are ranged against one another in the South African struggle for liberation. Is the enemy a monolith and will he remain so until his final defeat? What is the main content of the struggle for liberation and, flowing from this, which is the main revolutionary force and who are its potential allies and supporters? These are questions of capital importance. They play a vital part in determining the tactics of the revolutionary struggle, the broad alliances for which we must strive, the organisational structures we create and many other fundamental approaches. They must be considered within the framework of the special feature of the objective situation which faces us. South Africa's social and economic structure and the relationships which it generates are perhaps unique. It is not a colony, yet it has, in regard to the overwhelming majority of its people, most of the features of the classical colonial structures.

Conquest and domination by an alien people, a system of discrimination and exploitation based on race, technique of indirect rule; these and more are the traditional trappings of the classical colonial framework. Whilst at the one level it is an "independent" national state, at another level it is a country subjugated by a minority race. What makes the structure unique and adds to its complexity is that the exploiting nation is not, as in the classical imperialist relationships, situated in a geographically distinct mother country, but is settled within the borders. What is more, the roots of the dominant nation have been embedded in our country by more than three centuries of presence. It is thus an alien body only in the historical sense.

The material well-being of the White group and its political, social and economic privileges are, we know, rooted in its racial domination of the indigenous majority. It has resisted and will resist doggedly and passionately any attempt to shift it from this position. Its theorists and leaders ceaselessly play upon the theme of "We have nowhere else to go". They dishonestly ignore and even twist the fact that the uncertainty about the future of the oppressor in our land is an uncertainty born not of our racialism but of his. The spectre is falsely raised of a threat to the White men's language and culture to "justify" a policy of cultural discrimination and domination. By economic bribes and legal artifices which preserve for him the top layers of skills and wage income, the White worker is successfully mobilised as one of racialism's most reliable contingents. In every walk of life White autocracy creates privilege by operation of the law and, where necessary, the gun and with a primitive and twisted "proof" of its own superiority.

Nevertheless, the defence of all-round economic, social and cultural privileges combined with centuries of indoctrination and deeply felt theoretical rationalisation which centre on survival, will make the enemy we face a ferocious and formidable foe. So long as the threat from the liberation movement was not powerful enough to endanger the very existence of White *Baaskap* there was room for division – sometimes quite sharp in the White political camp.

Its motivation amongst the ruling class was competition for the lion's share of the spoils from the exploitation of the non-White people. It always centred around the problem of the most effective way of "keeping the native in his place". In such an atmosphere there were even moments when White workers adopted militant class postures against the small group which owns South Africa's wealth. But the changed world mood and internal situation inhibited these confrontations. The larger-minded White group as a whole moves more and more in the direction of a common defence of what is considered a common fate.

These monolithic tendencies are reinforced by a Hitler-like feeling of confidence that the fortress is impregnable and unassailable for all time. This process of all White solidarity will only be arrested by the achievements of the liberation movement. For the moment the reality is that apart from a small group of revolutionary Whites who have an honoured place as comrades in the struggle, we face what is by and large a united and confident enemy which is in alliance with, and is strengthened by world imperialism. All significant sections of the White political movement are in broad agreement on the question of defeating our liberation struggle.

This confrontation on the lines of colour – at least in the early stages of the conflict – is not of our choosing; it is of the enemy's making. It will not be easy to eliminate some of its more tragic consequences. But it does not follow that this will be so for all time. It is not altogether impossible that in a different situation the White working class or a substantial section of it, may come to see that their true long-term interest coincides with that of the non-White workers. We must miss no opportunity either now or in the future to try and make them aware of this truth and to win over those who are ready to break with the policy of racial domination. Nor must we ever be slow to take advantage of differences and divisions which our successes will inevitably spark off to isolate the most vociferous, the most uncompromising and the most reactionary elements amongst the Whites. Our policy must continually stress in the future (as it has in the past) that there is room in South Africa for all who live in it but only on the basis of absolute democracy.

So much for the enemy. What of the liberation forces? Here too we are called upon to examine the most fundamental features of our situation which serve to mould our revolutionary strategy and tactics. The main content of the present stage of the South African revolution is the national liberation of the largest and most oppressed group – the African people.

This strategic aim must govern every aspect of the conduct of our struggle whether it be the formulation of policy or the creation of structures. Amongst other things, it demands in the first place the maximum mobilisation of the African people as a dispossessed and racially oppressed nation. This is the mainspring and it must not be weakened. It involves a stimulation and a deepening of national confidence, national pride and national assertiveness. Properly channelled and properly led, these qualities do not stand in conflict with the principles of internationalism. Indeed, they become the basis for more lasting and more meaningful co-operation.

The national character of the struggle must therefore dominate our approach. But it is a national struggle which is taking place in a different era and in a different context from those which characterised the early struggles against colonialism. It is happening in a new kind of world – a world which is no longer monopolised by the imperialist world system; a world in which the existence of the powerful socialist system and a significant sector of newly liberated areas has altered the balance of forces; a world in which the horizons liberated from foreign oppression extend beyond mere formal political control and encompass the element which makes such control meaningful – economic emancipation. It is also happening in a new kind of South Africa; a South Africa in which there is a large and well developed working class whose class consciousness and independent expressions of the working people – their political organs and trade unions – are very much part of the liberation front. Thus, our nationalism must not be confused with chauvinism or narrow nationalism of a previous epoch. It must not be confused with the classical drive by an elitist group among the oppressed people to gain ascendancy so that they can replace the oppressor in the exploitation of the mass.

But none of this detracts from the basically national context of our liberation drive. In the last resort it is only the success of the national democratic revolution which – by destroying the existing social and economic relationships – will bring with it a correction of the historical injustices perpetrated against the indigenous majority and thus lay the basis for a new and deeper internationalist approach. Until then, the national sense of grievance is the most potent revolutionary force which must be harnessed. To blunt it in the interests of abstract concepts of internationalism is, in the long run, doing neither a service to revolution nor to internationalism.

The African although subjected to the most intense racial oppression and exploitation, is not the only oppressed national group in South Africa. The two million strong Coloured Community and three-quarter million Indians suffer varying forms of national humiliation, discrimination and oppression. They are part of the non-White base upon which rests White privilege. As such they constitute an integral part of the social forces ranged against White supremacy. Despite deceptive and often meaningless concessions they share a common fate with their African brothers and their own liberation is inextricably bound up with the liberation of the African people.

A unity in action between all the oppressed groups is fundamental to the advance of our liberation struggle. Without such a unity the enemy's strength multiplies and the attainment of a people's victory is delayed. Historically both communities have played a most important part in the stimulation and intensification of the struggle for freedom. It is a matter of proud record that amongst the first and most gallant martyrs in the armed combat against the enemy was a Coloured Comrade, Basil February. The jails in South Africa are a witness to the large-scale participation by Indian and Coloured comrades at every level of our revolutionary struggle. From the very inception of Umkhonto they were more than well represented in the first contingents who took life in hand to help lay the basis for this new phase in our struggle.

This mood was not only reflected in the deeds of its more advanced representatives. As communities too the Coloured and Indian people have often in the past, by their actions, shown that they form part of the broad sweep towards liberation. The first series of mass acts of deliberate defiance of the conqueror's law after the crushing of the Bambata rebellion, was the campaign led by that outstanding son of the Indian people – Mahatma Gandhi. Thereafter the Indian community and its leaders – particularly those who came to the fore in the 'forties – played no small part in the injection of a more radical and more militant mood into the liberation movement as a whole. The stirring demonstrations of the 'fifties from the Defiance Campaign to the Congress of the People, to the general strike, and the peasant revolts and mass demonstrations, saw many examples of united action by all the oppressed people. Indian workers responded in large numbers to almost every call for a general strike. Indian shopkeepers could always be relied upon to declare a day of hartal in solidarity with any protest which was being organised. Memory is still fresh of the outstanding response by the Coloured workers of the Western Cape to the 1961 call by the A.N.C. for a national general political strike.

The Alliance between the Congress organisations was a spur to the solidarity and reflected it. But events both before and after Rivonia put paid to the structures which had been created to express the Alliance.

How can we strengthen and make effective the cooperation between the communities and how can we integrate committed revolutionaries irrespective of their racial background?

Whatever instruments are created to give expression to the unity of the liberation drive, they must accommodate two fundamental propositions: Firstly, they must not be ambiguous on the question of the primary role of the most oppressed African mass and, secondly, those belonging to the other oppressed groups and those few White revolutionaries who show themselves ready to make common cause with our aspirations, must be fully integrated on the basis of individual equality. Approached in the right spirit these two propositions do not stand in conflict but reinforce one another. Equality of participation in our national front does not mean a mechanical parity between the various national groups. Not only would this in practice amount to inequality (again at the expense of the majority), but it would lend flavour to the slander which our enemies are ever ready to spread of a multi-racial alliance dominated by minority groups. This has never been so and will never be so. But the sluggish way in which the movement inside the country responded to the new situation after 1960 in which co-operation continued between some organisations which were legal (e. g. S.A.I.C., C.P.O., C.O.D.) and those that were illegal (e. g. A.N.C.) sometimes led to the superficial impression that the legal organisations – because they could speak and operate more publicly and thus more noticeably – may have had more than their deserved place in the leadership of the Alliance.

Therefore, not only the substance but the form of our structural creations must – in a way which the people can see – give expression to the main emphasis of the present stage of our struggle. This approach is not a pandering to chauvinism, to racialism or other such backward attitudes. We are revolutionaries, not narrow nationalists. Committed revolutionaries are our brothers to whatever group they belong. There can be no second class participants in our movement. It is for the enemy we reserve our assertiveness and our justified sense of grievance.

The important task of mobilising and gaining the support of other oppressed non-White groups has already been referred to. Like every other oppressed group (including the Africans) we must not naively assume that mere awareness of oppression will, by itself, push the Indian and Coloured people in the direction of opposing the enemy and aligning themselves with the liberation movement. The potential is there, because in a very real sense the future of the Indian and Coloured people and their liberation as oppressed groups is intimately bound up with the liberation of the Africans. But active support and participation have to be fought for and won. Otherwise the enemy will succeed in its never-ending attempt to create a gap between these groups and the Africans and even recruit substantial numbers of them to actively collaborate with it. The bottom of the barrel will be scraped in the attempt to create confusion about the objectives of the liberation movement. More particularly, the enemy will feed on the insecurity and dependency which is often part of the thinking of minority oppressed groups. He will try to raise a doubt in their minds about whether there is a place for them in a future liberated South Africa. The enemy has already spread the slander that at best for the Coloureds and Indians White domination will be replaced by Black domination.

It is therefore all the more important, consistent with our first principle, that the Coloured and Indian people should see themselves as an integral part of the liberation movement and not as mere auxiliaries.

Is there a special role for the working class in our national struggle? We have already referred to the special character of the South African social and economic structure. In our country – more than in any other part of the oppressed world – it is inconceivable for liberation to have meaning without a return of the wealth of the land to the people as a whole. It is therefore a fundamental feature of our strategy that victory must embrace more than formal political democracy. To allow the existing economic forces to retain their interests intact is to feed the root of racial supremacy and does not represent even the shadow of liberation.

Our drive towards national emancipation is therefore in a very real way bound up with economic emancipation.

We have suffered more than just national humiliation. Our people are deprived of their due in the country's wealth: their skills have been suppressed and poverty and starvation have been their life experience. The correction of these centuries-old economic injustices lies at the very core of our national aspirations. We do not underestimate the complexities which will face a people's government during the transformation period nor the enormity of the problems of meeting economic needs of the mass of the oppressed people. But one thing is certain – in our land this cannot be effectively tackled unless the basic wealth and the basic resources are at the disposal of the people as a whole and are not manipulated by sections or individuals be they White or Black.

This perspective of a speedy progression from formal liberation to genuine and lasting emancipation is made more real by the existence in our country of a large and growing working class whose class consciousness complements national consciousness. Its political organisations – and the trade unions have played a fundamental role in shaping and advancing our revolutionary cause. It is historically understandable that the doubly oppressed and doubly exploited working class constitutes a distinct and reinforcing layer of our liberation and socialism and does not stand in conflict with the national interest. Its militancy and political consciousness as a revolutionary class will play no small part in our victory and in the construction of a real people's South Africa.

Beyond our borders in Zimbabwe, Angola, Mozambique, Namibia are our brothers and sisters who similarly are engaged in a fierce struggle against colonialist and racist regimes. We fight an Unholy Alliance of Portugal, Rhodesia and South Africa with the latter as the main economic and military support. The historic ZAPU/A.N.C. Alliance is a unique form of co-operation between two liberation movements which unites the huge potential of the oppressed people in both South Africa and Zimbabwe. The extension of co-operation and co-ordination of all the people of Southern Africa as led by FRELIMO, ZAPU, SWAPO, M.P.L.A. and the A.N.C. is a vital part of our strategy.

What then is the broad purpose of our military struggle? Simply put, in the first phase, it is the complete political and economic emancipation of all our people and the constitution of a society which accords with the basic provisions of our programme – the Freedom Charter. This, together with our general understanding of our revolutionary theory, provides us with the strategic framework for the concrete elaboration and implementation of policy in a continuously changing situation. It must be combined with a more intensive programme of research, examination and analysis of the conditions of the different strata of our people, in particular those on the land, their local grievances, hopes and aspirations.

MICHAEL HARMEL: Born 1915, in Johannesburg; graduated in economics from Rhodes University, Grahamstown. From 1940–46, he was secretary of the Johannesburg District of the Communist Party; elected to the CP Central Committee, 1943; served as editor of the journals *Inkululeko* and *Liberation;* Johannesburg representative of *New Age;* and was secretary of the Transvaal Peace Council. In 1963 Mr. Harmel left South Africa while facing charges of breaking banning orders and worked in London as a free-lance journalist and later for *Problems of Peace and Socialism (World Marxist Review)* in Prague where he died in June, 1974.

THE COMMUNIST PARTY
OF SOUTH AFRICA

"... as I became more and more deeply involved with the Congress movement of those years, that is, the movement for freedom and equal human rights for all ... it was always members of the Communist Party who seemed prepared regardless of cost to sacrifice most; to give of their best, to face the greatest dangers, in the struggle against poverty and discrimination."

ABRAM FISCHER (Statement from the Dock: 28 March 1966)

"... for many decades Communists were the only political group in South Africa who were prepared to treat Africans as human beings and their equals; who were prepared to eat with us; talk with us, live with us and work with us. They were the only political group which was prepared to work with the Africans for the attainment of political rights and a stake in society. Because of this there are many Africans who today tend to equate freedom with Communism."

NELSON MANDELA (Speech in Court, June 1964)

In South Africa the Communist Party has long been known to the masses as a fearless and uncompromising fighter against fascist racism and terror. The trials in recent years of many of its leaders, Abram Fischer, Govan Mbeki, Ahmed Kathrada – together with many of their comrades of the African National Congress and other partners in the national liberation alliance, men such as Walter Sisulu, Nelson Mandela and many others, have brought home to millions of people in all five continents, the policy, character and calibre of the South African Communist Party.

In this, the land of apartheid, whose ruling classes have set themselves openly to implement the evil policy of apartheid – that is the deliberate cultivation of race and colour divisions and hatred, designed to perpetuate White privilege and domination – the Communist Party was and is a shining example of brotherhood and comradeship in the common cause. Included in its ranks, men and women of all the national groups that make up the population are joined in a spirit of equality and unity.

Twenty years ago the Nationalist Party government of South Africa brought in the Suppression of Communism Act (1950). This law declared the Communist Party of South Africa to be an illegal organisation, "and every branch, section or committee thereof". This vicious law has been properly described by the United Nations Unit on Apartheid as "the basic weapon in the armoury of apartheid". *(Repressive Legislation of the Republic of South Africa,* U.N. Publication ST/PSCA/SER.A/7, 1969.)

This law makes it a crime to "advocate, advise, defend or encourage" Communism or any of its objects. The "objects" of "Communism" are defined in such an extraordinary and all-embracing fashion that many people who are by no means Communists have been convicted and punished under it. For example, anyone who wants to bring about any "political, industrial, social or economic change" can be convicted of "statutory communism" if to obtain such a change he does – or even threatens to do – something illegal. In South Africa a man who threatened not to pay his taxes until the street lights were repaired could be found guilty of Communism. Penalty ten years jail.

But however widely its net has been spread – it has been amended more than 80 times since it was passed to make it more stringent and eliminate "loopholes" – the main target of this Act was and remains the Communist Party.

When one considers the nature, policy and record of the Communist Party over a half-century of unremitting struggle, it is not difficult to understand precisely why this Party was singled out as the central object of the hatred of the neo-Nazi Nationalist Party. For both in its theory – that of Marxism-Leninism, scientific socialism – and in its practice – unremitting and courageous work to organise and rally the masses in revolutionary struggle, the Communist Party stands for a policy directly opposed to that of the Nationalists.

Within six months of the establishment of the Communist Party on 30 July 1921 it was thrust by history into the midst of turbulent and far-reaching events.

The Witwatersrand (Transvaal) Strike of 1922 began as a strike of white coal miners against a pay cut; it rapidly developed into a strike on the gold fields which spread practically to the entire white working class of the Witwatersrand. It continued for three months, involving bloody armed clashes between the workers and the military before it was suppressed.

The bourgeois press called it "the Red Revolt". Smuts told his Parliament (19 March 1920) that "the aim of the Rand Revolutionaries was to establish a sort of Soviet Republic".

Of course, it was nothing of the sort. The organised white miners were striking against the introduction of "unqualified" (i. e. African) workers into certain skilled jobs which they had hitherto monopolised. The workers, many of them ex-servicemen, correctly assumed that Smuts would bring in troops to defend the mine owners and put down the strike. He had done it before – on the Witwatersrand in 1907, 1913 and 1914; and more recently in the Bulhoek (1920) and Bondelswart (1921) massacres.

They accordingly formed workers' commandos (combat divisions) for self-defence. The Smuts government forces used bombing aircraft, artillery, tanks, armoured trains, machine guns and rifles before the strikers were subdued. Over 250 lives were lost and thousands wounded. Over 1,000 strikers and their leaders were arrested; some like Long, Lewis, Fisher and Spendiff, were executed.

The onset of these momentous events placed the Communist Party in a difficult position. For years they had campaigned for the unity of the Black and White workers of South Africa; when the Africans at the mines came out on strike in 1920 they (then in the International Socialist League) had come out with their famous "Don't Scab!" leaflet calling on the white miners to stand by their fellow workers. The issue upon which the Chamber of Mines had precipitated the strike was the very one most certain to split the workers and rouse antagonism on both sides. Nor – though the Chamber's motive was merely to make bigger profits by more intensive exploitation of Black labour –

could it be denied that the colour bar was in itself immoral and reactionary. Bill Andrews, who was to become one of the most prominent of the militants in the strike, had written to a friend when it broke out, "My private opinion is that it will inevitably be lost; it is ... impossible for the white workers in South Africa permanently to keep the natives out of any form of industry they are capable of undertaking."

Yet the Communist Party could not by any means take a detached view. The great majority of its members were militant leaders in the existing movement of white labour; they could not stand aside from a major clash between their fellow workers and the major imperialist concentration in the country, backed by the viciously reactionary Smuts government. The Party and its members proved themselves the most disciplined and devoted militants during the course of strike, while never ceasing for a moment from their propaganda that it was the Chamber of Mines and the government who were the enemy, not the African fellow workers of the strikers. It was mainly due to their work that apart from one or two untypical incidents, the government never succeeded in provoking clashes between the white and black workers during the strike.

The strike was, as Andrews had predicted, lost. But at the General Election of 1924 the South African Party of Smuts paid the penalty for the brutal methods of its repression. Hated by all sections of the working population, it was defeated by the "Pact" alliance of the old Nationalist Party under General Hertzog and the Labour Party.

The Labour Party, in the face of vigorous criticism from the C.P.S.A. – though it supported the anti-Smuts alliance in the elections – accepted a few positions in the Hertzog government, thereby becoming a junior partner in the landowner capitalist administration. The white workers were conceded a legally privileged position, in colour bars for the mines and in the industrial legislation of the country; emasculating the militancy and class-consciousness of their trade union and their Labour Party. For the next fifty years they failed to play any significant part independent of the imperialist-dominated state structure of which they regarded themselves as a part.

The Communist Party absorbed the profound lessons of these events. They dropped their formal proposal to affiliate to the Labour Party, turned their attention increasingly towards the tasks of organising and raising the socialist consciousness of the African workers, the true propertyless proletarians of the country, and of establishing co-operative and fraternal relations with the African National Congress and other liberation movements of the oppressed peoples.

An irreplaceable part was played by the Party and its members in building the I.C.U. (Industrial and Commercial Workers' Union), the first mass trade union of African workers, whose dramatic growth and influence was a remarkable phenomenon of the 'twenties. Though the general secretary, Clements Kadalie, was a powerful orator, he lacked organising experience and political understanding, qualities evidenced by James La Guma, E. J. Khaile, John Gomas and other Communist and left-wing militants in the leadership and rank and file of the I.C.U. From small beginnings the I.C.U. spread "like a veld fire" among the urban and rural members until its membership topped the hundred thousand mark and the organisation became a powerful factor in the land. At a time when the A.N.C. was undergoing a temporary eclipse it put forward political demands, such as the abolition of pass laws, as well as demands for better pay and conditions, and even the leaders of the White political parties, such as the Nationalist and Labour Parties, had to pay heed to the I.C.U. Unfortunately internal differences arose. Communists and others demanded a more militant policy of action, as well as proper accounting for funds and collective leadership. As a result of these differences, as well as outside pressures from liberals and the International Federation of Trade Unions who persuaded him that if he could get rid of the "extremists" and stick to "sane trade unionism" the organisation would be recognised by the government, Kadalie embarked on a purge of the Communists and succeeded in getting a majority of the Executive to debar Party members from holding office in the I.C.U. The new course proved disastrous for the organisation, and before long the I.C.U. declined and disintegrated. But its pioneering propaganda and organisation had done a great deal to awaken the Africans for the struggles of the future.

The Communist Party turned towards the organisation of African workers into industrial trade unions which won many benefits for their members and continued to do so until the increasingly terrorist actions of the Nationalist government made open trade unionism virtually impossible in the 'sixties.

Many members of the trade unions were brought into the night schools established by the Party to combat illiteracy and develop socialist consciousness. A storming campaign was carried out among the rural masses by S. P. Bunting, for election as "Native Representative" in Parliament for the Tembuland constituency in 1929. Although harassed continually by police, government agents and white hooligans, he succeeded in conveying the Party's message – equality, land, freedom and majority rule – to millions of peasants.

As a result of these and other militant activities among the oppressed majority, many of them rallied to the Party's banner during the 'twenties, including such outstanding personalities as Albert Nzula (the first African to become General Secretary of the Party), Moses Kotane, Johannes Nkosi, Gana Makabeni, J. B. Marks, E. T. Mofutsanyana: men who left their mark in the revolutionary labour and liberation movements.

Thus the Party entered the 'thirties with greatly increased strength and influence among the masses. It played a militant and leading role in the fight against the pass laws, the reactionary anti-African legislation of the Hertzog-Pirow government, the attempts to place the brunt of the world-wide economic crisis on the backs of the workers. The Party organ *Umsebenzi* (The Worker) carried on the fight, in various African languages, on these issues, against the Italian fascists' invasion of Ethiopia, and the growing menace of fascism at home and abroad and against the danger of world war. In the trade union movement, Party members of the calibre of Bill Andrews, Makabeni, I. Wolfson and W. Kalk, in the Transvaal, Ray Alexander in the Cape, H. A. Naidoo in Natal, strove tirelessly to organise both white and non-white workers.

Thus the 'thirties witnessed an increasingly sharp clash between the reactionary Hertzog-Smuts government on the one hand and the forces of democracy and freedom, in which the Communist Party suffered heavy blows. Following the murder of Johannes Nkosi the police, especially in Natal, launched a wave of terror which forced it into semi-illegality. The Party fought back valiantly. A joint demonstration of white and non-white unemployed invaded the Rand Club in Johannesburg – "the millionaires' club" – and demanded to be served with a meal; they were served, but it cost the organiser, I. Diamond, a stretch in the Fort Prison. J. B. Marks was "nominated" as a Parliamentary candidate in the Germiston by-election in 1932 – of course as an African he was not eligible, but it was an effective demonstration for African franchise rights.

This period also, however, saw the emergence of an "ultra-left", sectarian tendency at the head of the Party's administration. This tendency was not confined to South Africa: a number of the fraternal Parties affiliated to the Comintern, and under the influence of its executive, made similar errors at the time. The results were particularly unfortunate for the C.P.S.A.: a wave of highly undemocratic and arbitrary expulsions took place, whose victims included two of the veteran founders, S. P. Bunting and Bill Andrews. Kotane was removed from the editorship of *Umsebenzi*.

The seventh and last world congress of the Communist International in 1935 emphasised the urgency of striving for broad united fronts of the workers and democrats everywhere against the menace of fascism and war. It was a rebuff for "ultra-left" and sectarian policies, and its adherents departed from the scene. Andrews was reinstated in the Party, and tributes – unhappily posthumous – paid to the outstanding contribution of S. P. Bunting. But the ideological and personal disputes lingered on, especially at the Party's headquarters in Johannesburg. Activity declined, and the Party's organ, *Umsebenzi*, was compelled to close down for lack of funds.

At the beginning of 1939, following a special conference, it was decided to transfer the site of the executive to Cape Town where Moses Kotane, Bill Andrews, Ray Alexander and other senior members were living. With Kotane as General Secretary and Andrews as Chairman a new beginning was made on the patient and methodical rebuilding of the Party structure. Himself a staunch member of the African National Congress, Kotane placed great emphasis on the task of building a united front of the Party, the A.N.C. and other democratic, working class and liberation movements for the winning of political, economic and social equality for all South Africans as the prime task for the advance to socialism.

Relationships between the A.N.C. and the Communist Party had fluctuated in previous periods. Following a visit to Belgium, as delegate to the International Congress against Colonial Oppression and Imperialism held in Brussels in 1927, the A.N.C. President J. T. Gumede had been invited to visit the Soviet Union. He was deeply impressed by what he had seen. "I have seen the new world where it [the revolution] has already begun. I have seen the new Jerusalem," he declared, and he proposed A.N.C. co-operation with the Communists of South Africa, "the only Party which stood by us and protested when we have been shot down." But the conservative elements were not prepared to accept his radical and militant ideas; he was defeated when he stood for re-election at the A.N.C. national conference of 1930, and relationships between the two organisations temporarily deteriorated.

In Johannesburg, a new district committee elected at the beginning of 1940, succeeded in uniting and mobilising the Party and healing past rifts. A new Party journal, *Inkululeko* (Freedom) published in English, Sesotho, Tswana, Zulu, Xhosa, Venda and Tsonga won widespread readership and support from the Africans for its vigorous policies of working class and national advance. Under the editorship of E. T. Mofutsanyana, it proved a worthy successor to *The International* and *Umsebenzi*. Vigorous efforts were made to organise the African Mine Workers' Union under the dynamic leadership of J. B. Marks and the peasants, especially in the Zoutpansberg, through the efforts of Alpheus Maliba and others.

Similar progress was scored in other industrial areas, notably Durban, where well-known Indian trade unionists such as H. A. Naidoo and G. Ponen played a notable part and in Port Elizabeth, under the leadership of Gladstone Tshume, Raymond Mhlaba and other worker-militants of the trade union movement and the A.N.C.

The Nazi attack on the Soviet Union in June 1941 brought about a transformation in the international situation. The character of the Second World War was altered, for the workers of the world could not stand aside when the first workers' state was in peril. The Smuts government paid lip-service to the war effort but in practice it refused to mobilise the non-White majority by giving them rights to defend, or to train and arm African soldiers to play their part in the common victory. The Party fought vigorously for the abolition of pass laws and other oppressive legislation, for democratic changes in the country's constitution and for the suppression of pro-Nazi groups within the country.

These tireless campaigns, as well as the heroic example of a socialist state in arms provided by the Soviet Union, brought a new accession of strength and influence from all sections of the population to the Communist Party of South Africa and its policy of people's unity for a democratic South Africa and for victory. Thousands of votes were cast for African Communists such as E. T. Mofutsanyaya and A. Maliba in such token "elections" as were still permitted by the South African constitution at that time. Militants such as Drs. Naicker and Dadoo were elected at the head of the Indian Congress. The Communist candidate, Sam Kahn, was elected as African representative of the Cape Western constituency to Parliament and his colleague Fred Carneson to the Provincial Council, as were several Party candidates to the Cape Town City Council, where Coloured men still had a share of the vote. Even the all-white electors of Hillbrow elected Hilda Watts as the first (and to date the only) Communist Party representative on the Johannesburg City Council, and under a leadership which included Communist servicemen like Jack Hodgson and Cecil Williams the Springbok Legion was joined by tens of thousands of serving soldiers.

The Party's policy of democratic unity proved successful. The widespread anti-pass campaign of 1943 was led by a united front committee under the leadership of Dr. A. B. Xuma, A.N.C. president general, after having been launched by a provisional committee headed by Dr. Dadoo. Under the dynamic leadership of Dr. Dadoo, then president of the South African Indian Congress, the Indians launched on a courageous campaign of resistance against Smuts' segregation plans – "the Ghetto Bill", with the four-square support of the A.N.C. With the ending of the war in Europe a great demonstration of over 20,000 was held in Johannesburg under the joint leadership of the A.N.C., the Transvaal Indian Congress, the A.P.O.,* the Council of Non-European Trade Unions and the Communist Party.

A major turning point was the great African mine workers' strike of August 1946. Every difficulty had been put in the way of the A.M.W.U. (African Mine Workers' Union) by the government and the Chamber of Mines. Union organisers were forbidden access to the mine compounds; an "Emergency War Measure" – prolonged long after the end of the war – made it illegal to hold meetings in the vicinity of the mines. Nevertheless organisation spread steadily. The workers were furiously indignant at their bad and dangerous conditions and their wretched rates of pay – they demanded a minimum of ten shillings a day. The Chamber refused to meet union leaders or even to acknowledge their letters and memoranda. The workers decided to strike, and over 100,000 came out for one week before the strike was brutally suppressed by armed police in actions which cost hundreds in killed and wounded. Thousands of Union members were victimised and the compounds were saturated with hundreds of spies and informers.

During the latter war years, participation in the anti-fascist war in which the principal part was played by the Socialist Soviet Union, had led to certain minor modifications of the normal despotic rule that prevails in South Africa – as it must in a society where four-fifths of the population is denied citizenship rights. The "Native Affairs" Minister, Deneys Reitz, had temporarily suspended some of the applications of the pass laws (they were soon restored by his successor, van der Byl). It is true that *Inkululeko* was withheld from its readers outside the Rand by a secret ban imposed through the post office, and

* African People's Organisation of mainly Coloured (mixed origin) membership.

216

Party members continued to be harassed by the Special Branch of the police. But it is also true to say that never before nor since had the Party won, through mass support and correct strategies, so substantial a measure of the concession to work as a legally permitted political Party.

It was a short-lived and temporary respite.

Hardly had the miners' strike begun in 1946 when massive police raids took place throughout the country on the Party premises and on the offices and homes of its more prominent personnel. Thousands of documents were confiscated. The entire membership of the Johannesburg District Committee was arrested and charged with the leaders of the African Mine Workers' Union and others. They were charged – together with Dr. Dadoo, then Chairman of the District Committee, who was then serving a sentence as an Indian Congress resister and Moses Kotane who was in Cape Town throughout the strike – with "sedition" and assisting an illegal strike. They were convicted on the second charge. The sedition accusation was dropped, or so it seemed. Within months the Central Executive Committee of the Party was arrested and accused of the same offence – sediton – in a marathon trial that dragged on until late in 1948 before it was finally dropped by the state. Until the Treason Trial of the 'fifties it was the longest political trial in the country's history.

The African miners' strike heralded a new round of sharp confrontations between the ruling classes, on the one hand, and the oppressed people and their organisations on the other.

The lesson was not lost on the people's leaders. The year 1947 saw the conclusion of the "Xuma-Dadoo-Naicker" pact for the united struggle of the A.N.C. and the S.A.I.C. (South African Indian Congress) – the cornerstone of the famous "Congress Alliance" which was to emerge in the 'fifties as the most formidable opposition to fascism and the only basis for a real resistance and challenge to White supremacy in South Africa.

The democratic majority of South Africans was deeply shocked by the election victory in 1948, of the alliance of Malan's and Hertzog's Afrikaner Nationalist Parties (later to fuse into one) over Smuts's United Party. Though there was little love for Smuts, the henchman of the mine owners and of British imperialism, the Nationalists were clearly the most chauvinist and bitter enemies of the non-White majority, of democracy and freedom. Deeply infected with Hitler's Nazi ideas, they had worked for an Axis victory during the war, and were sworn to "destroy" Communism.

The Communist Party courageously rallied the workers and democratic forces. "We are not afraid of the threats of the Nationalists" declared a Party pamphlet (*Malanazi Menace*), issued immediately after the election. *The Guardian, Inkululeko, Fighting Talk*, and other progressive journals ceaselessly appealed for unity and resistance. These calls did not go unheeded. On 1 May 1950 the vast industrial complex of the Witwatersrand came to a halt in response to a call for a general strike, for freedom of speech, movement and organisation, issued jointly by the African and Indian Congresses, the African People's Organisation, the Council of Non-European Trade Unions and the Communist Party. The government's reaction was to ban all demonstrations and police opened fire on a number of young Africans in the streets of Alexandra Township.

It was against this background of growing unity and mass militancy that the Nationalist Minister of Justice, Swart, introduced into Parliament his Unlawful Organisations Bill – subsequently named the Suppression of Communism Act, which has been briefly described at the outset of this paper. The terms of this legislation were such that anyone who had ever been a member or supporter of the Party, even though he had done nothing illegal at the time, was automatically placed upon a special list, making him automatically subject to penalties and restrictions by Ministerial decree, without any right of appeal to the courts.

Unfortunately this legislation was brought in at a time which found the Central Executive of the Party unprepared, either practically or psychologically, to face the complexities and rigours of underground work. For a decade its energies had been concentrated on establishing, through mass work in the name of the Party, protracted court proceedings and participation in the various public elections open to it, the right of the Communist Party to function as a public political organisation, the only non-racial Party in the country. Among the leadership were some who doubted the possibility, others even the necessity, for it to maintain its vanguard role even under conditions of illegality.

The reaction of the Central Committee to the Bill – at a specially convened meeting in June 1950 – was to decide, by majority vote – to dissolve the Party. There are still some, notably Professor Simons, himself a leading Central Committee member at the time, who have attempted to justify this decision on the grounds of expediency. *(Colour and Class in South Africa,* 1970). Dealing with this question the 1962 Programme of the South African Communist Party declares that "legalistic errors" had penetrated the ranks of the Party which was "unprepared and unwilling to work underground. These errors culminated in the dissolution of the Party."

The Communists, despite innumerable restrictions and bans placed upon them by the government, continued to work valiantly in the national liberation and trade union movements for those immediate aims common to all their members. Communists set an outstanding example of loyal and devoted work in all the great united campaigns of the Congress movement in the 'fifties.

Immediately the terms of the "Unlawful Organisations Bill" became known, the African National Congress summoned an emergency conference in Johannesburg, to which were invited the Indian Congress, the A.P.O., the Council of Non-European Trade Unions (all of whom accepted), the Trades and Labour Council and the Labour Party (who did not). In the light of the Bill, the May Day shootings and numerous other repressive acts of the government it was decided to call a one-day general strike all over the country on 26 June 1950 – the origin of what has become South Africa's *Freedom Day*.

The Fighting Fifties were a memorable decade in the history of the liberation struggle in South Africa, marked by repeated national general strikes, the famous Campaign of Defiance of Unjust Laws (1952), the great drive of mass education and activity that preceded and accompanied the Congress of the People and the adoption of the Freedom Charter (1955). These were the years of the Treason Trial, the peasant revolts in Sekhukhuniland, the Transkei and elsewhere, the "£1-a-day" campaign of the Congress of Trade Unions; the years of the mass bus boycotts in Alexandra Township and elsewhere, of the splendid demonstrations against the extension of the pass laws led by the Women's League of the A.N.C. backed by the non-racial Federation of South African Women.

In all of these campaigns the names of South African Communists such as J. B. Marks, Moses Kotane, Dr. Dadoo, Bram Fischer, Govan Mbeki, Brian Bunting and many another were ever prominent, side by side with those of great leaders like Chief Lutuli, Nelson Mandela, Walter Sisulu, Dr. Naicker.

It was the period of which Bram Fischer had written: "It was always members of the Communist Party who seemed prepared, regardless of cost, to sacrifice most; to give of their best, to face the greatest dangers."

It had been not long after the dissolution of the Party in 1950 that experience had proved the absolute indispensability of its existence. However devoted the work of individuals, and whatever the difficulties and dangers that had to be faced, the collective leadership of a Marxist-

Leninist vanguard was essential in the course of the national liberation struggle. Accordingly, the steeled leading cadres of the movement, together with new forces which had arisen in the course of the struggle, came together to establish the South African Communist Party: the inheritors and continuers of the movement which had been established by Andrews, Jones and Bunting in 1915, and consolidated in the establishment of the Communist Party of South Africa in 1921.

During the long course of its history, the South African Communist Party has undergone a striking process of evolution and development. Beginning as it did long ago, within the heart of the organised and predominantly white labour movement at the birth of the Union of South Africa, step by step it was transformed into a Party reflecting the national character of the predominantly African population, and stood in the forefront of what has become a protracted, armed struggle for national liberation from White domination and apartheid.

This process was accompanied, not without internal pangs and conflicts, by a steady ideological growth, with the aid of Marxist-Leninist science and the assistance of the Communist International, towards an integrated understanding of the character of the country and the theory of the South African Revolution.

In its earlier period, the Party tended strongly to apply to South African conditions the ideas, programmes and slogans of West European and North American Marxists. But their conditions were totally different. It is true that, no sooner were the Party's founders liberated from the stultifying opportunism of the Social-Democratic Labour Party, than they began to turn their attention to the major question of the growing African proletariat; towards socialist education and organisation among these workers. Their main concern, however, at first, was to include the African workers in the working class struggle for socialism as an immediate aim in which the already organised trade union movement was seen as the potential leading revolutionary force. Even after the bitter experiences of the 1922 strike and the Nationalist-Labour government, such ideas stubbornly persisted, although they were decisively defeated at the Party's 1924 Congress.

An important step forward was marked by the Sixth Congress of the Comintern, where after the problems of South Africa were discussed in a special commission, the slogan was advanced (against the incorrect arguments put forward at that time by the C.P.S.A. delegation) of an independent African republic, as a stage towards a workers' and peasants' socialist government. The overall concept was posed as the national liberation struggle of the African and other oppressed peoples of South Africa.

This process of theoretical clarification was greatly amplified and filled in by the Programme *The Road to South African Freedom,* unanimously adopted by the Fifth National Conference to be held underground by the South African Communist Party in 1962.

The introduction boldly launches into the very heart of the problem:

"Our country, South Africa, is known throughout the world because of its system of White domination, a special form of colonialism which has been carried to extremes under the Nationalist Party policy of apartheid. Nowhere else is national and racial oppression practised so nakedly and shamelessly, with such systematic brutality and disregard of human rights and dignity."

The 1962 Programme places in the forefront the "immediate and foremost task" of the Party to "work for a united front of national liberation ... for a national democratic revolution to destroy White domination"; a revolution whose "main content will be the national liberation of the African people" but which, "carried to its fulfilment" will at the same time put an end to every sort of race discrimination and privilege ... restore the land and wealth to the people and guarantee democracy, freedom and equality of rights to all . . ."

"The destruction of colonialism and the winning of national freedom is the essential condition and the key for future advance to the supreme aim of the Communist Party; the establishment of a socialist South Africa, laying the foundation of a classless, communist society."

The Programme sums up, for a generation of South Africans who have been cut off from open education in scientific socialist principles, the fundamentals of Marxism-Leninism, of Marxist dialectical and historical materialism, the essence of capitalist exploitation, the nature of modern imperialism as analysed by Lenin, the October Revolution and the essentials of proletarian internationalism in the world of today.

It sets the South African situation in its geographical and historical environment – the African Revolution against imperialism, for independence throughout the continent; the "Colonialism of a Special Type" which has grown up in our country as a result of the incursions of the Boer settlers and then of British imperialism.

"South Africa is not a colony but an independent state. Yet the masses of our people enjoy neither independence nor freedom. The conceding of independence to South Africa by Britain, in 1910, was not a victory over the forces of colonialism and imperialism. It was designed in the interests of imperialism. Power was transferred not into the hands of the masses of people of South Africa, but into the hands of the White minority alone. The evils of colonialism, in so far as the non-White majority was concerned, were perpetuated and reinforced. A new type of colonialism was developed, in which the oppressing White nation occupied the same territory as the oppressed people themselves and lived side by side with them."

The rapid process of industrialisation within the country has tremendously accelerated the process of differentiation and imbalance in the country's social structure, concentrating great wealth and profits in the upper strata of the Whites, intensifying the deprival of the non-Whites. It has created the material basis for the phenomenon of "apartheid" – of "two South Africas".

On one level, that of "White South Africa", there are all the features of an advanced capitalist state in its final stage of imperialism. There are highly developed industrial monopolies, and the merging of industrial and finance capital. The land is farmed along capitalist lines, employing wage labour, and producing cash crops for the local and export markets. The South African monopoly capitalists, who are closely linked with British, United States and other foreign imperialist interests, export capital abroad, especially in Africa. Greedy for expansion, South African imperialism reaches out to incorporate other territories – South-West Africa and the Protectorates.

But on another level, that of "Non-White South Africa", there are all the features of a colony. The indigenous population is subjected to extreme national oppression, poverty and exploitation, lack of all democratic rights and political domination by a group which does everything it can to emphasise and perpetuate its alien "European" character. The African Reserves show the complete lack of industry, communications, transport and power resources which are characteristic of African territories under colonial rule throughout the continent. Typical, too, of imperialist rule, is the reliance by the state upon brute force and terror, and upon the most backward tribal elements and institutions which are deliberately and artificially preserved. Non-White South Africa is the colony of White South Africa itself.

It is this combination of the worst features both of imperialism and of colonialism, within a single national frontier, which determines the special nature of the South African system, and has brought upon its rulers the justified hatred and contempt of progressive and democratic people throughout the world.

It is within this context then that the Programme analyses the "forces of change"; the class and national forces whose unity is essential to bring about freedom. The White aristocracy of labour cannot be regarded as the moving force of the democratic revolution; sharing in the super-profits of the monopoly bourgeoisie derived from a colonial-type exploitation they have become in that sense their junior partners, though their permanent and long term interests lie in unity against the common exploiter.

At the present stage then the revolutionary forces consist in the African people, headed by the revolutionary working class in close alliance with the oppressed rural masses and the Coloured and the Indian people. These masses, the great majority of South Africans, have built up their traditional liberation movements – the African National Congress, the Indian Congress and the Coloured People's Congress. The democratic section of the whites have also their part to play. The determined and experienced working class of South Africa has its own class organisations: the Congress of Trade Unions and the workers' party – the South African Communist Party.

All these organisations have already formed a stable and principled alliance – the Congress Alliance. They have hammered out a common political programme: the Freedom Charter.

In its own Programme, the Communist Party explicitly endorses the Freedom Charter, "which the Party considers to be suitable as a general statement of the aims of a national democracy." It is then within the framework of the Charter that the Party advanced its own immediate proposals.

These call for a unitary South African state with a republican form of government; all legislative bodies to be elected by "equal, direct adult franchise without regard to race, colour, sex, property, educational or other qualifications."

The Party calls for the fullest freedom of thought and speech, but warns that the utmost vigilance "must be exercised against those who would seek to organise counter-revolutionary plots, intrigues and sabotage ... to restore White colonialism and destroy democracy."

In the sphere of economic development, the Party advocates large-scale planned development controlled and directed by the state; mining, banking and monopoly industries to be nationalised.

Land in the possession of monopolies, absentee owners, employers of convict or indentured labour and other "idlers, exploiters and parasites" is to be confiscated and placed in the hands of those who live and work on the land.

Finally, in the field of external relations, the Programme calls for peaceful coexistence of states with different social systems, universal disarmament and internationalism. It proclaims the principles of self-determination and African unity, pledges help to African states "in their struggles to liberate themselves from colonialism"; calls for the strengthening of ties and brotherhood among the people of the whole world.

The 1962 Programme of the Stormy Sixties also marked a new stage in the assessment of the strategy and methods of struggle of the period ahead. The slogan of "non-violence" which had served the democratic movement in the 'fifties was considered "harmful to the cause of the national democratic revolution in the new phase of the struggle, disarming the people in the face of the oppressor."

The correctness of this conclusion was fully borne out during the Stormy Sixties which saw one brutal blow after another delivered against the masses by the fascist government. The African National Congress was banned outright after half a century of legal existence, in 1960. Introducing unlimited detention without trial, torture and murder in the prison cells, the police struck savagely against the liberation movement.

The Communist Party and its cadres together with their comrades in arms of the united liberation movement suffered severely. Among the innumerable Congress leaders, such as Mandela and Sisulu (life sentences), Mini, Khayinga, Mkaba (executed), Babla Saloojee (murdered by police) and many others, many Communists like Govan Mbeki, Ahmed Kathrada, Bram Fischer have been sentenced to life imprisonment; others have fallen in the struggle on battlefield or prison cell.

Against this terror the liberation movement, including the Communist Party, have struck back in armed conflict.

Today all sections of consistent democrats in our country are agreed that there is no way out but the revolutionary way; the path of armed struggle.

The year 1970 saw an important event in the life of the Party: its Augmented Central Committee, which reviewed and reassessed its policy and activity and renewed its leadership. It issued a rousing Call to the South Africans – a call which concludes:

Today at this critical time, the Communist Party calls on you. It calls on all South Africans who love their country and who love freedom. We call upon the workers and the people in the countryside. We call upon the African people, the Coloured people, the Indians and the democratic elements among the whites.

Let us build up our people's organisations, in town and country, in factories, mines and villages.

Let us unite for the fight to end the shame and suffering of White minority rule headed by the Nazi Nationalist Party.

Let us resolve that the beginning of the 'seventies will put an end to White South Africa and mark the beginning of People's South Africa, advancing towards socialism.

The armed groups of *Umkhonto we Sizwe* are ready to enter the fight. But they cannot fight alone.

The people must act!

They must build and support their illegal organisations, the A.N.C., the trade unions and the Communist Party.

They must act militantly for higher wages, land and freedom.

They must arouse the spirit of resistance and defiance.

They must arm themselves.

The war of national liberation is on and we must fight it to the finish.

Victory or death!

An analysis of The Freedom Charter, the Revolutionary Programme of the African National Congress, as presented at the Morogoro Conference, Tanzania, May 1969.

THE FREEDOM CHARTER

The South Africa of today is the product of the common labour of all its peoples. The cities, industries, mines and agriculture of the country are the result of the efforts of all its peoples. But the wealth is utilised by and for the interests of the White minority only.

The African National Congress was formed in 1912 to unite the Africans as a nation and to forge an instrument for their liberation. From the outset the African National Congress asserted the right of the African people as the indigenous owners of the country, entitled to determine its direction and destiny. Simultaneously our forefathers recognised that the other groups in the country, the Europeans, Indians and Coloureds were historically part and parcel of South Africa.

The A.N.C. rejected the claims of the European settlers to domination, and fought against all attemps to subjugate them in the land of their birth. But in the face of the gravest injustices the A.N.C. never once abandoned the principle that all those who had their home in the country of the Africans, were welcome, provided only that they accepted full and consistent equality and freedom for all. In this the A.N.C. was not merely bowing to history and reality but believed that it was correct in principle to make this position clear. Over and over again in the face of manifest inhumanity the A.N.C. absolutely refused to be provoked into abandoning its democratic principles.

The ruling White minority rejected the concepts of the A.N.C. and to that extent the movement and the people fought and will fight them.

In the early 'fifties when the struggle for freedom was reaching new intensity the need was seen for a clear statement of the future South Africa as the A.N.C. saw it. Thus was born the Congress of the People Campaign. In this campaign the African National Congress and its allies invited the whole of South Africa to record their demands which would be incorporated in a common document called the Freedom Charter. Literally millions of people participated in the campaign and sent in their demands of the kind of South Africa they wished to live in. These demands found final expression in the Freedom Charter. The Freedom Charter was adopted at the Congress of the People representative of all the people of South Africa which met at Kliptown, Johannesburg on 25 and 26 June 1955. The three thousand delegates who gathered at Kliptown were workers, peasants, intellectuals, women, youth and students of all races and colours. The congress was the climax of the campaign waged by the African National Congress, the South African Indian Congress, the Coloured People's Organisation, the South African Congress of Trade Unions and the Congress of Democrats. Subsequently all these organisations adopted the Freedom Charter in their national conferences as their official programme. Thus the Freedom Charter became the common programme enshrining the hopes and aspirations of all the progressive people of South Africa.

Today the African National Congress and its allies are engaged in an armed struggle for the overthrow of the racist regime. In its place the A.N.C. will establish a democratic state along the lines indicated in the Freedom Charter. Although the Charter was adopted fourteen years ago its words remain as fresh and relevant as ever. Some who have forgotten its actual terms or the kind of document it is, who detach this or that phrase from the document taken as a whole, imagine that the conditions of armed struggle somehow invalidate some provisions of the Charter. What we believe is that the Charter may require elaboration of its revolutionary message. But what is even more meaningful, it requires to be achieved and put into practice. This cannot be done until state power has been seized from the fascist South African government and transferred to the revolutionary forces led by the A.N.C.

The Preamble of the Freedom Charter

The first lines of the Charter declare that South Africa belongs to all who live in it, Black and White, and that no government can justly claim authority unless it is based on the will of the people.

The expression "South Africa belongs to all who live in it, Black and White" embodies the historical principle which has characterised the policy of the African National Congress towards the peoples who have settled in the country in the past centuries. The African people as the indigenous owners of the country have accepted that all the people who have made South Africa and helped build it up, are components of its multi-national population, are and will be in a democratic South Africa, and people inhabiting their common home. No government can justly claim authority unless it is based on the will, not just of the Whites, but of all the people of the country. The Freedom Charter thus begins by an assertion of what is and has been a cardinal democratic principle, that all can live in South Africa whatever their origin, in equality and democracy. That the South Africa of the future will not be a country divided unto itself and dominated by a particular racial group. It will be the country of all its inhabitants. It is the White people who, in the past as now, have rejected this principle leaving the people no alternative but to convince them by the truth of revolutionary struggle. The Preamble ends by calling on the people, Black and White, as equals, country-men and brothers to pledge to strive together sparing neither strength nor courage until the democratic changes set out in the Freedom Charter had been won.

The Preamble couched in terms similar to many famous documents reflecting man's aspiration for freedom called for a new state resting on the will of the people – a repudiation of the existing state and a call for revolution. Hereunder we examine, briefly, each section of our Charter.

The People Shall Govern!

The Republican constitution of South Africa passed in 1961 is a monument to racialism and despotism. In terms of this constitution supreme legislative authority is vested in the White fascist State President, the House of Assembly and the Senate. Only a White person can be elected State President. The House of Assembly and the Senate consist exclusively of White representatives elected by an exclusively White electorate. Therefore the power to make laws in our country is a monopoly of the White minority.

The same applies to other organs of government such as the four provincial councils of Natal, Cape, Orange Free State and Transvaal which are headed by a White Administrator assisted by an all White Executive Council. Organs of local government such as District Councils, Municipal Councils, boroughs are manned entirely by White people. Such organs of local government as there are for non-Whites consist of the Transkei Legislative Council and an Executive; the Indian Council; the Coloured Council; urban Bantu Authorities, Territorial Authorities and other such bodies. These are all undemocratic institutions with little or no power and serving merely as a sounding board for the White minority government.

The administration in South Africa is similarly manned at all significant levels by White persons.

A successful armed revolution will put an end to this state of affairs.

The Parliament of South Africa will be wholly transformed into an Assembly of the People. Every man and woman in our country shall have the right to vote for and stand as a candidate for all offices and bodies which make laws. The present administration will be smashed and broken up. In its place will be created an administration to which all people irrespective of race, colour or sex can take part. The bodies of minority rule shall be abolished and in their place will be established democratic organs of self-government in all the provinces, districts and towns of the country.

All National Groups Shall Have Equal Rights!

In South Africa not only does the system at present enforce discrimination against individuals by reason of their colour or race but in addition some national groups are privileged, as such, over others. At the moment the Afrikaner national group is lording it over the rest of the population with the English group playing second fiddle to them. For all the non-White groups – the Africans, Indians and the Coloureds – the situation is one of humiliation and oppression. As far as languages are concerned only Afrikaans and English have official status in the bodies of state such as Parliament or Provincial Councils; in the courts, schools and in the administration. The culture of the African, Indian and Coloured people is barely tolerated. In fact everything is done to smash and obliterate the genuine cultural heritage of our people. If there is reference to culture by the oppressors it is for the purpose of using it as an instrument to maintain our people in backwardness and ignorance.

Day in and day out White politicians and publicists are regaling the world with their theories of national, colour and racial discrimination and contempt for our people. Enshrined in the laws of South Africa are a host of insulting provisions directed at the dignity and humanity of the oppressed people.

A democratic government of the people shall ensure that all national groups have equal rights, as such, to achieve their destiny in a united South Africa.

There shall be equal status in the bodies of state, in the courts and in the schools for the Africans, Indians, Coloureds and Whites as far as their national rights are concerned. All people shall have equal right to use their own languages, and to develop their own folk culture and customs; all national groups shall be protected by laws against insults to their race or national pride; the preaching and practice of national, racial or colour discrimination and contempt shall be a punishable crime; and all laws and practices based on apartheid or racial discrimination shall be set aside.

The People Shall Share in the Country's Wealth!

Today most of the wealth of South Africa is flowing into the coffers of a few in the country and others in foreign lands. In addition the White minority as a group have over the years enjoyed a complete monopoly of economic rights, privileges and opportunities.

An A.N.C. government shall restore the wealth of our country, the heritage of all South Africans to the people as a whole. The mineral wealth beneath the soil, the banks and monopoly industry shall be transferred to the ownership of the people as a whole.

At the moment there are vast monopolies whose existence affects the livelihood of large numbers of our people and whose ownership is in the hands of Europeans only. It is necessary for monopolies which vitally affect the social well-being of our people such as the mines, the sugar and wine industry to be transferred to public ownership so that they can be used to uplift the life of all the people. All other industry and trade which is not monopolistic shall be allowed with controls to assist the well-being of the people.

All restriction on the right of the people to trade, to manufacture and to enter all trades, crafts and professions shall be ended.

The Land Shall Be Shared
Among Those Who Work It!

The indigenous people of South Africa after a series of resistance wars lasting hundreds of years were deprived of their land. Today in our country all the land is controlled and used as a monopoly by the White minority. It is often said that 87 per cent of the land is "owned" by the Whites and 13 per cent by the Africans. In fact the land occupied by Africans and referred to as "Reserves" is state land from which they can be removed at any time but which for the time being the fascist government allows them to live on. The Africans have always maintained their right to the country and the land as a traditional birthright of which they have been robbed. The A.N.C. slogan *Mayibuye i Afrika* was and is precisely a demand for the return of the land of Africa to its indigenous inhabitants. At the same time the liberation movement recognises that other oppressed people deprived of land live in South Africa. The White people who now monopolise the land have made South Africa their home and are historically part of the South African population and as such entitled to land. This made it perfectly correct to demand that the land be shared among those who work it. But who works the land? Who are the tillers?

The bulk of the land in our country is in the hands of land barons, absentee landlords, big companies and state capitalist enterprises. The land must be taken away from exclusively European control and from these groupings and divided among the small farmers, peasants and landless of all races who do not exploit the labour of others. Farmers will be prevented from holding land in excess of a given area, fixed in accordance with the concrete situation in each locality. Lands held in communal ownership will be increased so that they can afford a decent livelihood to the people and their ownership shall be guaranteed. Land obtained from land barons and the monopolies shall be distributed to the landless and land-poor peasants. State land shall be used for the benefit of all the people.

Restrictions of land ownership on a racial basis shall be ended and all land shall be open to ownership and use to all people, irrespective of race.

The State shall help farmers with implements, seeds, tractors and dams to save soil and assist the tillers. Freedom of movement shall be guaranteed to all who work on the land. Instruments of control such as the "Trek Pass", private gaols on farms, forced labour shall be abolished. The policy of robbing people of their cattle in order to enforce them to seek work in order to pay taxes shall be stopped.

All Shall Be Equal Before the Law!

In terms of such laws as the notorious Suppression of Communism Act; the Native Administration Act; the Riotous Assemblies Act; the Terrorism and Sabotage Acts and many other laws, our people suffer imprisonment, deportation and restriction without fair trials. These laws shall be abolished. No one shall suffer imprisonment, deportation or restriction without a fair trial.

In our country petty government officials are invested with vast powers in their discretion to condemn people. These powers shall be ended.

The courts of South Africa are manned by White officials, magistrates, judges. As a result the courts serve as instruments of oppression. The democratic state shall create courts representative of all the people.

South Africa has the highest proportion of prisoners of any state in the world. This is because there are so many petty infringements to which a penalty of imprisonment is attached. In a new South Africa, imprisonment shall only be for serious crimes against the people, and shall aim at re-education, not vengeance.

It has been a standing policy of White governments in South Africa to prevent Africans and other non-Whites from holding responsible positions in the police force. The present police force and army are instruments of coercion to protect White supremacy. Their whole aim is punitive and terroristic against the majority of the population.

It is the major aim of the armed revolution to defeat and destroy the police force, army and other instruments of coercion of the present state.

In a Democratic South Africa the army and police force shall be open to people of all races. Already *Umkhonto*

We Sizwe – the nucleus of our future people's army – is an armed force working in the interest of people drawn from the land for their liberation. *Umkhonto We Sizwe* consists of people drawn from all population groups in South Africa.

All Shall Enjoy Equal Human Rights!

South Africa has numerous laws which limit or infringe the human rights of the people. One need only mention the notorious Suppression of Communism Act; Proclamation 400 which imposes a state of emergency in the Transkei; the Proclamation of 1953 which bans meetings of more than ten Africans in scheduled areas; the Native Laws Amendment Act which introduces racial discrimination in churches and places of worship; the Bantu Education Act which makes education without a government permit an offence – surely an offence unique in the world – to educate without a permit!

All the above Acts and regulations will be swept away by a people's government. The laws shall guarantee to all their right to speak, to organise, to meet together, to publish, to preach, to worship and to educate their children.

The Pass Laws of South Africa result in the arrest of an average of 1,100 persons a day. These laws control and prohibit movement of our people in the country. There are also laws which restrict movement from one province to another. As part of their checking of the people numerous police raids are organised during which homes are broken into at any time of the day or night. Many laws give the police powers to enter people's homes without warrant and for no apparent reason except to terrorise them.

All this shall be abolished. The privacy of the home from police raids shall be protected by law.

All shall be free to travel without restrictions from

countryside to town, from province to province and from South Africa abroad.

Pass laws, permits and all other laws restricting these freedoms shall be abolished.

There Shall Be Work and Security!

As with everything else the rights of collective bargaining of workers in South Africa have been twisted and warped by racial ideas and practices. Africans do not have the right to form registered trade unions and are prohibited from going on strike. Other workers are forced to belong to racially divided unions. The government has the power to determine what jobs shall be reserved for what racial groups. People of different races are paid differential wage rates for the same work. Migratory labour is a chief feature of the South African economy and leads to massive social upheaval and distress particularly among Africans. In the Democratic State the A.N.C. is determined to achieve, all who work shall be free to form trade unions, to elect their officers and to make wage agreements with their employers.

The State shall recognise the right and duty of all to work and to draw full unemployment benefits. Men and women of all races shall receive equal pay for equal work. There shall be a forty-hour working week, a national minimum wage, paid annual leave, sick leave for all workers and maternity leave on full pay for all working mothers. Miners, domestic workers, farm workers, and civil servants shall have the same rights as all others who work to form trade unions, and join political organisations.

The use of child labour, the housing of male workers in single men's compounds, the system whereby workers on wine farms are paid tots of wine as part payment on their wages, contract labour – all these pernicious practices shall be abolished by a victorious revolutionary government.

The Doors of Learning and Culture Shall Be Opened!

One of the biggest crimes of the system of White supremacy is the damage it has done to the development of the people of South Africa in the fields of learning and culture. On the one hand the minds of White people have been poisoned with all manner of unscientific and racialist twaddle in their separate schools, colleges and universities. There has been made available to them all the worst forms of so-called Western culture. The best creations of art, writing, the theatre and cinema which extol the unity of the human family and the need for liberty are only made available in dribs and drabs, whilst the general position is one of a cultural desert. As far as the non-White people are concerned the picture is one of deprivation all along the line. One has to think hard to discover whether or not there is even one single theatre, drama school, ballet school, college of music to which non-Whites are admitted in South Africa. In Cape Town there is some ridiculously slight opening for Coloured people. Otherwise 8 per cent of the people of South Africa are by and large confined to the few cinemas whose fare is the most inferior type of American cinema art.

A vigilant censorship system exists to ensure that these racially separate cinemas do not show non-Whites anything that is considered to be bad for them by the authorities.

It is not only that non-Whites are virtually debarred from the cultural productions of mankind, but in addition everything has been done to prevent them developing their own national cultures. Publishing is strictly controlled. Apart from the most banal forms of music, the people are not encouraged or allowed to produce such music as enhances their spirit. Such music as contains protest against conditions of life are searched for and prohibited. The languages of the people are not permitted to be developed by them in their own way. Ignorant and officious White professors sit in education committees as arbiters of African languages and books without consultation with the people concerned. The grotesque spectacle is seen of the White government of South Africa posing as a "protector" of so-called Bantu culture and traditions of which they know nothing. The arrogance of the fascists knows no bounds! They apparently love African culture more than the Africans themselves! The truth is that they wish to preserve these aspects of the African tradition which contain divisive tendencies likely to prevent the consolidation of the African people as a nation.

The forces represented in the present state after combating education of non-Whites for over one hundred years suddenly decided to take over all education as a state responsibility. The result was the introduction of a racially motivated ideological education; a lowering of standards; the emergence of tribal colleges; and the intensification of racial separation in university education. Science and technology are hardly taught to non-Whites. The training of doctors and other medical personnel is derisory.

The Democratic State shall discover, develop and encourage national talent for the enhancement of our cultural life; all cultural treasures of mankind shall be open to all, by free exchange of books, ideas and contact with other lands. The aim of education shall be to teach the youth to love their people and their culture, to honour human brotherhood, liberty and peace.

Education shall be free, compulsory, universal and equal for all children.

Higher education and technical training shall be opened to all by means of state allowances and scholarships awarded on the basis of merit.

Adult illiteracy shall be ended by a mass state education plan.

Teachers shall have the rights of other citizens to organise themselves and participate in political life. The colour bar in cultural life, in sport and education shall be abolished.

There Shall Be Houses, Security and Comfort!

Migratory labour and its concomitant of separation of families, social problems and distress, is one of the tragedies of South Africa. Residential segregation is the order of the day throughout South Africa. Massive shortage and bad housing for non-Whites and huge homes and flats most of which are either empty or not fully used for the White minority. The infant mortality rate in our country is among the highest in the world, and the life expectancy of Africans among the lowest. Medical services are haphazard and costly.

The Democratic State established after the victory of the revolution shall ensure the right of the people to live where they choose, to be decently housed, and to bring up their families in comfort and security. The vast unused housing space in such areas as the flatlands of Hillbrow and Johannesburg shall be made available to the people. Rent and prices shall be lowered, and adequate amounts of food shall be made available to the people. A preventive health scheme shall be run by the state. Free medical care and hospitalisation shall be provided for all, with medical care for mothers and young children. Slums, which have to some extent been demolished in the nine major centres of the country, shall be eliminated in the middle of towns and rural areas where the majority of the people live.

New suburbs shall be built where proper facilities shall be provided for transport, lighting, playing fields, crèches and social centres.

The aged, the orphans, the disabled and the sick shall be cared for by the state.

Every person shall have the right to leisure, rest and recreation.

Fenced locations, and racial ghettoes shall be abolished and laws which result in the breakup of families shall be repealed.

There Shall Be Peace and Friendship!

In the wake of the victorious revolution a Democratic People's Republic shall be proclaimed in South Africa. This shall be a fully independent state which respects the rights and sovereignty of nations.

South Africa shall strive to maintain world peace and the settlement of international disputes by negotiation – not war.

Peace and friendship amongst all people shall be secured by upholding the equal rights, opportunities and status of all.

The Democratic State shall maintain close neighbourly relations with the states of Lesotho, Botswana and Swaziland in place of the present veiled threats and economic pressure applied against our brothers and sisters in these states by White supremacy.

Democratic South Africa shall take its place as a member of the O.A.U. and work to strengthen Pan-African unity in all fields. Our country will actively support national liberation movements of the peoples of the world against imperialism and neo-colonialism.

Diplomatic relations will be established with all countries regardless of their social and political systems on the principles of mutual respect for each other's independence, sovereignty and territorial integrity.

The economic and cultural interests of those countries which sympathise with and support the struggle of South Africa for freedom shall be respected.

The revolutionary struggle is in its infancy. It will be a long hard road. To accomplish the glorious task of the revolution maximum unity among all national groups and revolutionary forces must be created and maintained. All

South African patriots whatever their race must take their place in the revolution under the banner of the African National Congress. Forward to revolution and the victory of the people's programme of liberation!

GEORGE SHEA: African National Congress militant, somewhere in Africa. His poetry has been included in *Poems for Our Revolution*.

FRONT LINE

Front-line
Where manhood and consciousness is tested
The only place to bury persecutions and burden of ages

The only place to declare names immortal
Trust me brother you will not be alone there.

Front-line
Where bullets will graze on man and grass
Where man will make his own lightning and thunder
Where the enemy will fall and never to rise
Brother truly my shadow will be next to yours.

Front-line
I know it is bitter but I like it
I like it particularly because it is bitter
I like it because it is where I belong
For out of bitterness comes equality, freedom and peace.

I will be in the front-line when the roll is called

Front-line valleys and plains of events and history.

Briefly,
ABOUT THE EDITOR

Alex La Guma, born 1925 in Cape Town, was on the staff of *New Age* 1955–62. He took a leading part in preparations for the Congress of the People which met at Kliptown, Johannesburg, in 1955, to draw up the historic declaration of rights, the Freedom Charter. In 1956, he was one of 156 men and women of all races who stood trial on a charge of treason. Five years of legal argument and political struggle ensued before charges were thrown out of court. In 1960, after the Sharpeville massacre, he was again detained for five months. In December, 1962, Alex La Guma was confined to house arrest for five years. Nothing that he said or wrote could be reproduced in South Africa. In 1963 and 1966, he was twice detained without trial and held in solitary confinement. In 1966, he left South Africa and now lives in London with his family. His three novels, *A Walk in the Night* (Mbari Publications, Nigeria, 1962), *And A Threefold Cord* (1964), and *The Stone Country* (1967), the latter two published by Seven Seas Books, were written under house arrest. Alex La Guma was awarded the 1969 Afro-Asian Lotus Prize for Literature. His fourth novel, *In the Fog of the Season's End,* was published by Heinemann Educational Books (1972).

A brief biography of each author appears above the article, essay or poem which make up this volume.